Creativity in Church Management

Creativity in Church Management

Entrepreneurship for a 21st-Century Parish

Best Practices in Church Management

Edited by Charles E. Zech

Paulist Press
New York / Mahwah, NJ

Cover image (background): lmichman/bigstock.com
Cover & book design by Dawn Massa, Lightly Salted Graphics

Library of Congress Cataloging-in-Publication Data
Names: Zech, Charles E., 1947– author.
Title: Creativity in church management : entrepreneurship for a 21st-century parish / edited by Charles E Zech.
Description: New York / Mahwah, NJ : Paulist Press, [2021] | Series: Best practices in church management | Summary: "An auxiliary contribution to the Best Practices in Church Management series, this book contains material from presentations at two International Festivals of Creativity in Church Management, one held at the Lateran University in Rome, the other at Villanova"— Provided by publisher.
Identifiers: LCCN 2020037802 (print) | LCCN 2020037803 (ebook) | ISBN 9780809155453 (paperback) | ISBN 9781587689437 (ebook)
Subjects: LCSH: Church management.
Classification: LCC BV652 .C685 2021 (print) | LCC BV652 (ebook) | DDC 254—dc23
LC record available at https://lccn.loc.gov/2020037802
LC ebook record available at https://lccn.loc.gov/2020037803

ISBN 978-0-8091-5545-3 (paperback)
ISBN 978-1-58768-943-7 (e-book)

Published by Paulist Press
997 Macarthur Boulevard
Mahwah, New Jersey 07430
www.paulistpress.com

Printed and bound in the
United States of America

Contents

About the Series

"The church is not a business!" Those of us who are involved in church management hear this comment on a regular basis. The appropriate response is, "Yes, it's true that the church is not a business, but we do have a stewardship responsibility to use our resources effectively. Frequently, that responsibility requires the utilization of sound business management techniques."

Canon law lists three priestly functions. Priests are responsible for teaching, sanctifying, and governing. Most priests relish their roles as teachers and sanctifiers, but few priests get excited over the parish governance tasks that are their responsibility. Very few men seek ordination because they want to run a small business.

While a parish isn't a business, governing a parish requires a significant number of management skills. Funds must be raised and bills must be paid, presumably under the guidance of a parish budget. Staff must be hired and provided with direction. The significant investment in parish facilities needs to be properly maintained. Church security, regarding both facilities and personnel, has become increasingly important. Parish planning is an ongoing requirement. The pastor is expected to show leadership in a variety of areas. The list goes on. All these activities must be carried out within the constraints posed by both canon and civil laws.

In fact, the task of governing a parish has become even more challenging in recent years. Because of a number of factors, men are often assigned to administer larger and more complex parishes. Some are assigned as pastor of multiple parishes. In some cases, these multiple parishes are a great distance from one another. And in far too many cases, we are asking our priests to live alone.

Unfortunately, our seminaries are so overwhelmed with the educational requirements necessary to turn out priests that they are unable to make room in the curriculum to educate them as pastors. This may not have been a serious concern when the church was flush with priests and men would spend fifteen to twenty years serving as parochial vicars, in effect serving as apprentices and learning how to govern a parish. Today, however, it is not unusual for a priest to be assigned his first pastorate two or three years after ordination.

The good news is that, in many cases, pastors are assisted by a lay staff. But often the lay staff members themselves lack management training. They too struggle with budgets, managing volunteers, conflict resolution, planning for the future, and other management tasks.

Paulist Press has recognized the need for a series of educational materials to address the needs of church workers, both clergy and staff, who serve in a variety of management roles ranging from parishes to dioceses to social service organizations and who have no previous management experience. The result is this series on Best Practices in Church Management.

This series of books covers a wide range of functional church management areas, presented at a level of understanding intended for those church workers who find themselves with management responsibilities but little or no management education or experience. These are practical guides to parish management, not academic treatises. Jargon has been eliminated. Their purpose is to remove the anxiety from church management. These are the books that could be used in a seminary short course on parish management or presented to a newly appointed pastor. Parish, diocesan, and social service staff members with a background in areas such as theology, education, or social work who have suddenly been thrust into a management role will also find this series useful. Even those with some management background will appreciate the detailed discussions they will find in these books.

I am proud to be working with Paulist Press as the Best Practices in Church Management series editor. Paulist Press has a well-established reputation for turning out the finest in educational materials to serve the church. This series is no exception. We have been able to attract national experts in each of a variety of functional management fields to share their wisdom. We hope you will find each book to be an invaluable guide as you carry out your stewardship in service to the church.

Charles E. Zech, PhD
Professor Emeritus of Church Management
Villanova University

Preface

The International Festivals of Creativity in Church Management

Charles E. Zech

As we move through the twenty-first century, the global Catholic Church is experiencing some significant changes. Some of these are the result of dynamics outside of the church's direct control, while others find their source in circumstances that are the consequence of church activities. All require some out-of-the-box thinking and creative solutions on the part of church leadership. They include the following:

1. A massive geographic shift of the world's Catholic population. In the United States the shift has involved the movement of Catholics from the Northeast and Midwest to the South and West, and from the inner city to the suburbs. Globally, the growth in the Catholic Church has been imbalanced, with growth occurring primarily in Africa and Latin America.

2. This shift in population has been accompanied by a mismatch of church resources. In the United States, most of the priests and parishes are still located in the Northeast and Midwest and in the inner cities. Globally, while two-thirds of the world's Catholics reside outside of North America and Europe, they are served by only one-third of the priests.

3. This mismatch is accompanied by a declining number of priests along with an aging priesthood. The result is an increasing workload for our priests. In the United States in 2012 there were 1,728 Catholics per priest, up from 900 in 1982.[1] The ratio is far worse in Africa and Latin America.

4. Underlying all of this is the threat of church finances. In the United States, where parishes rely on voluntary parishioner contributions, Catholics are notoriously low givers. The typical Catholic household contributes only about 1.1 percent of its income to the parish, compared with the 2.2 or 2.3 percent that Protestants contribute to their congregations. In Europe, some countries (e.g., Germany and Italy) fund their churches through national taxes based on church membership, but as fewer people declare their membership, church revenues decrease.

As a result of these changes there is considerable pressure to foster more effective church management skills:

1. As a result of the shifting population trends and the declining number of priests, dioceses have been required to reconfigure their parish organizational structures, consolidating parishes in some places and utilizing innovative staffing options. Among those available through canon law are appointing laypeople to administer

parishes (can. 517.2) or assigning a priest to pastor more than one parish (can. 526.1). These innovative parish organizational structures are accompanied by their own sets of issues.

2. Also related to the declining number of priests is an increased reliance on paid laypeople and unpaid lay volunteers to staff parish ministries, although these both probably would have occurred based on Vatican II's call for laity to live out their baptismal vows through active participation in parish life. According to Allen,[2] the Catholic Church's workforce grew from 1.6 million in 1978 when Pope John Paul II was elected to 4.3 million in 2005 when he died, 90 percent of whom are laity. In the United States there are more paid lay parish employees than there are diocesan priests.[3] This raises the issues of the need to effectively manage them and fairly compensate them.

3. The demand on the part of the nonstaff laity to be involved in diocesan and parish decision-making processes through regular forums such as advisory councils (diocesan and parish pastoral councils and diocesan and parish finance councils), along with extraordinary events like diocesan synods to live out their baptismal vows.

4. The need to change the pattern of low levels of Catholic contributions to their parish in order to properly maintain the large amount of physical structures that the church owns and pay lay staff a just wage. The impact of low giving makes the threat of reduced government support in some countries even more pronounced.

5. The need for seminaries to educate their students to be pastors, not just priests. Priests have the threefold ministry of teaching, sanctifying, and governing. Governing is typically the area where our priests have received the least amount of training, where their skill set is least likely to reside, and where they need the most assistance. The days when a young priest could expect to spend ten to fifteen years in apprenticeship before being appointed a pastor are behind us. Many priests are assigned their first pastorate two to three years after ordination.

Creative ideas are needed at every level as the church manages these changes, ranging from the way it educates its clergy and lay leaders to the way it structures and leads our parishes to the way dioceses are administered. All the while we must continue to heed Pope Francis's admonition, "Mere administration can no longer be enough. Throughout the world let us be permanently in a state of mission."[4]

As the church continues to grapple with these issues, our understanding of their underlying nature and available solutions must continue to evolve. A key factor in this evolution is the impact of research. Evidence-based knowledge creation continues to be essential. Furthermore, we need to use our research to identify creative solutions to the many issues facing the twenty-first-century church.

To that end, the Center for Church Management at Villanova University partnered with the International School of Pastoral Management at Pontifical Lateran University in Rome to sponsor two conferences on the topic of Creativity in Church Management. On March 23–25, 2017, the First International Festival of Creativity in Church Management (subtitled "What Kind of Church in 20 Years?") was held at the Pontifical Lateran University in Rome. The Second International Festival of Creativity in Church Management (subtitled "The Entrepreneurial Spirit in a Mission-Driven Church") was held at Villanova University near Philadelphia on June 25–27, 2018.

These were truly international events, attended by church leaders from twenty-five countries representing six continents. They included church hierarchy, clergy, and involved lay leaders. Some

Creativity in Church Management: Entrepreneurship for a 21st-Century Parish

of the best church researchers from around the globe presented their creative ideas for church management. Topics covered ranged from creative ideas on diocesan governance to parish administration to seminary education and included presentations on innovative approaches to pastoral planning, church finances, and parish reconfiguration, among others.

The events were billed as "Festivals" rather than conferences because there were multiple opportunities for the attendees to be proactive and to interact with the presenters and with one another. Time was set aside for any participant to present his or her original ideas or project on specific areas of interest. Exhibits by organizations engaged in best practices were available throughout the Festivals. The fact that the papers were presented by some of the top researchers of church management issues in the world, and that they have been revised based on feedback from participants from around the globe, has ensured that the chapters in this book represent thinking that rises above the parochial interests of any one geographical region.

This book reports on the findings of the Festivals by presenting some of the research papers that were presented at both Festivals. Two of the papers in this volume were presented at the First International Festival and eight were presented at the Second International Festival. They were all revised and improved upon based on comments received from Festival participants.

Chapter Summaries

This book on creative solutions to parish management begins appropriately with a chapter by Rev. William Clark, SJ, "Communities of Living Faith: Parish Management and Theological Discernment."

Fr. Clark sets the stage for a discussion of parish management by introducing the reader to an ecclesial perspective of Catholic parishes, citing canon 515 of the Code of Canon Law. As Fr. Clark notes, canon law speaks of the parish as a stable community of the faithful, entrusted to a pastor, and connected to the universal church. Fr. Clark then goes on to cite scriptural references that serve as the theological grounding for the parish as viewed in canon law. All of the chapters that follow should be viewed in the context of Fr. Clark's opening comments on what is consistent with church teachings.

Fr. Clark's chapter is followed by four chapters discussing creativity in parish leadership.

In "What Do You Mean, *Co-Responsible*? Leadership in a Co-Responsible Parish," based on a paper presented at the First International Festival, Marti Jewell delves into a concept that was popularized by Pope Benedict XVI in his address delivered at the 2009 Opening of the Pastoral Convention of the Diocese of Rome at the Basilica of St. John Lateran.

Jewell examines co-responsibility from the perspective of three styles of pastoral leadership:

- Leaders who feel responsible for the community and responsible to their superiors
- Leaders focused on working with a core team, sharing in providing programs and services to the parish
- Leaders where pastor and team focus on animating the community for missionary discipleship

Professor Jewell argues for a team-based, shared leadership of pastor and staff, recognizing that leadership is not an individual endeavor but rather depends on mutual interdependence as pastor and staff work toward the same goal: establishing a "total ministering community."

Mark Mogilka's chapter, "Parish Pastoral Leadership: The Challenge of Fostering Unity While Nurturing Diversity," is also based on a paper that was presented at the First International Festival. It addresses issues faced by leaders in multicultural parishes, consolidated parishes, those in a multiparish pastoring situation, those torn between generational differences or theological differences, and those led by international priests. Pastors in these situations are charged with promoting unity in the parish while cultivating the diverse and unique groups that comprise the parish community and can be a source of strength. Fostering unity, Mogilka asserts, citing Pope Francis, is not the same as uniformity. Rather, it is the recognition and acceptance of the various gifts that each member brings and enabling them to place these gifts at the service of all members of the parish community. In other words, it is based on the ecclesiology of the church as the Body of Christ. He goes on to offer a number of practical and creative suggestions on how the church can foster unity while nurturing diversity.

Christian Olding, Thomas Suermann de Nocker, and Maximilian Warmbrunn wrote a chapter based on their presentation at the Second International Festival titled "The Entrepreneurial Spirit in a Mission-Driven Church: Administration for a Pastoral Future." In their paper they use the unique German model of top-down financing to address the issue of creativity in pastoral support. In the German model, church revenues are collected by the government through the taxing mechanism, which then distributes funds directly to dioceses. The dioceses in turn then distribute funds to their parishes. Since administrative and pastoral content are interrelated, the diocese plays a large role in influencing and supporting pastoral work. This centralized system enables diocesan leaders to gather innovative ideas from across the diocese and disseminate them to pastors throughout the diocese.

In a chapter based on a paper that was presented at the Second International Festival, "Silent Contracts: Implicature, Parish Leadership Style, and Parishioner Engagement," Marti Jewell examines how the implicit, unspoken, and unexamined contracts between parishioners and parish leaders shape the life of the parish. Parish leaders and parishioners are called to work together to renew pastoral structures to make them more mission oriented, ultimately leading to more open and inclusive pastoral activities.

The next three chapters are concerned with some important aspects of the reconfiguration of parish organizational structures. As described earlier in this introductory chapter, a number of forces are at work that require dioceses to implement new organizational structures for their parishes, other than the arrangement of a priest pastor residing in each parish. These three chapters address some of the overlooked features of parish organizational structure reconfiguration.

In "Ministry and Sacramentality in Faith Communities without Resident Priest Pastors," presented at the Second International Festival, Peter Gilmour discusses innovative ways for a parish to thrive when it lacks a resident priest. These include home-based rituals, local devotions, base communities, pilgrimages, street processions, and other sacramental practices that don't necessarily require the presence of a priest. There are many ways that parishioners can express their Catholicism, Gilmour argues. Diversity, not uniformity, is the future of the church.

Mark Mogilka's chapter presented at the Second International Festival, "New Metrics and Processes for Evaluating Parish Consolidations," uses a case study of a parish consolidation to argue that, in order to adequately assess a consolidated parish, multiple perspectives, strategies, and new metrics, are needed. It is important that we not only listen to leadership but also sample parishioners to learn of their perceptions, hopes, and dreams. The outcome should be a situation where dialogue and discernment occur between and among parish leaders, parishioners, and diocesan leaders resulting in the creation of a strategic pastoral plan.

Tobias Schuckert's presentation at the Second International Festival resulted in his chapter "Francis Xavier`s Intercultural Principles and Global Entrepreneurship of the Church in the Twenty-

First Century." In this time when Catholic parishes are becoming more multicultural as parishes are reconfigured, especially in the United States, there are some important lessons to be learned from the evangelization efforts of Francis Xavier. As he ministered in the Far East, he had to change his mindset from a methodology that had worked in Western Europe to one that paid respect to the culture and religious traditions of the culture he was evangelizing. From Francis Xavier's life, Schuckert identifies five principles that are relevant for the mission of the church in the twenty-first century as the church reaches out to a multicultural society.

Issues concerned with creativity in functional areas of church management are addressed in the next two chapters.

"Ecclesiastical Crowdfunding: An Innovative Form of Church Financing," by Christoph Biermeier, is based on his presentation at the Second International Festival. Biermeier looks to the social media mechanism of crowdfunding as a potential source of revenue for parishes wishing to finance special projects. In addition to its financial potential, crowdfunding can help the parish form a new relationship with potential members.

Declan Cahill's chapter, "The 'Two-Hat' Theory of Management: A Pastor's Role in Performance Management," is based on a presentation at the Second International Festival. In it, he tackles the tricky question of performance management of church workers. While few may relish the task of evaluating the performance of their subordinates, it is a necessary evil. Every worker deserves to learn how well their superior believes they are performing, but this task is even more complicated for pastors, since they wear two hats: they are both managers and spiritual leaders. To resolve this conflict Cahill presents ten "Performance Management Principles."

Finally, the book ends with a summary chapter.

Conclusion

While the other books in this series each focus on a single functional church management issue, this book considers a variety of church management topics that while important, would not warrant coverage by an entire book. It is intended to fill in some cracks in the coverage of church management. The chapters contained in this book provide an overview of the types of creative thinking that the church is going to need as well as creative guidelines for how the church should proceed as it moves through the twenty-first century. The chapters contain many commonalities:

- The importance of ensuring that all church management activities are grounded in sound theology
- The role of sound stewardship in employing church resources
- The importance of forming clergy who are both creative thinkers and committed to a co-responsible style of leadership
- The importance of the laity themselves stepping forward to take on a co-responsible role

The bottom line is that, while the church is not a business, it does have a stewardship responsibility to use its resources effectively. Typically, this involves the use of sound management techniques, adapted to the special needs of a faith-based organization. As a human institution, it must acclimate to changing conditions in order to survive. This is a continuous process.

Notes

1. Charles E. Zech, Mary L. Gautier, Mark M. Gray, Jonathan L. Wiggins, Thomas P. Gaunt, SJ, *Catholic Parishes of the 21st Century* (New York: Oxford University Press, 2017), 22.

2. John Allen, *The Future Church: How Ten Trends Are Revolutionizing the Catholic Church* (New York: Doubleday, 2009), 195.

3. Zech, et al, *Catholic Parishes*, 42.

4. Francis, Apostolic Exhortation *Evangelii Gaudium,* §25. http://w2.vatican.va/content/francesco/en/apost_exhortations/documents/papa-francesco_esortazione-ap_20131124_evangelii-gaudium.html.

Acknowledgments

The chapters in this book are revisions of papers presented at two international conferences, referred to as "Festivals" because of the high level of both formal and informal interaction between presenters and attendees. The Festivals were co-sponsored by the Center for Church Management at Villanova University in the United States and the International School of Pastoral Management at the Pontifical Lateran University in Rome. On March 23–25, 2017, the first "International Festival of Creativity in Church Management: What Kind of Church in 20 Years?" was held at the Pontifical Lateran University. Giulio Carpi, the Director of the International School of Pastoral Management, served as the primary organizer of this Festival. Matthew Manion, Faculty Director and James Gallo, Director of the Center for Church Management were primarily responsible for organizing the second "International Festival of Creativity in Church Management: The Entrepreneurial Spirit in a Mission-Driven Church," held June 25–27, 2018, at Villanova. Twenty-five countries and six continents were represented at the two Festivals.

A number of church management scholars who presented papers at the two Festivals are not included in this volume. Nevertheless, they made important contributions through their comments on the chapters that substantially contributed to the revisions that appear in this volume. They included Robert Dixon, Rev. Brian Lucas, and Gabrielle McMullan, all from Australia; Benedikt Jürgens, Stefan Korta, Rosel Oehmen-Vieregge, Bernd Halfar, Lucas Wehner, and Linda Dürrich, from Germany; Veronica Carpi, Rev. Franco Finocchio, Rev. Cristian Mendoza, and Paolo Cortellessal, from Italy; Madalena Eça de Abreu from Portugal, Rev. Jordi Pujol, Rev. Diego Zalbidea, and Juan Luis Martinez, from Spain; and Mary Gautier, Rev. Stephen Fichter, and Bryan Froehle, from the United States.

Finally, a great deal of thanks goes to our editor at Paulist, Donna Crilly, who went well beyond the usual duties of an editor by her ability to take chapters written by a variety of authors, for some of whom English is a second language, with each writing in a separate format, and putting them into a consistent format.

1

Communities of Living Faith

Parish Management and Theological Discernment

William A. Clark, SJ

In the leadership of Catholic parishes, it is tempting to proceed as if basic questions of the mission and identity of any local Catholic church community were already settled, fully determined by church law and custom. If that were true, parish leaders would be free simply to seek out creative approaches to the tasks and functions that come with that predetermined identity. However, the complexities hiding within the simple question, "What *is* a parish, anyway?" are still often left unattended,[1] lost in the rushing current of parish life, even though attention to them would allow a more coherent understanding of the tasks and functions.

In a general way, of course, the mission is indeed established, as the canonical description of the parish makes clear: a parish is "a certain community of the Christian faithful stably constituted in a particular church" (can. 515). What, though, is implied by that beautiful and carefully chosen term, "community of the Christian faithful"?[2] If we give every word of this legal definition its full weight, it presents the parish as a living, dynamic sharing of life and love (communion) through, with, and in Christ. Because of this bond, Christ constantly reveals the Father to us amid and even through our ongoing relationships, practices, and ways of pursuing our Christian faith. If this is so, an authentic understanding of a particular parish's mission and identity requires more than simply understanding the words of the Code of Canon Law. What is further needed is real engagement in an ongoing process of discernment, continually bringing together the functions of responsible church management with practical theological questions (Christian reflection on ongoing community experience), in a complementary and creative relationship. Failure to recognize this dynamic can allow us to drift toward standards and "best practices" that were developed for other situations, that do not heed the voice of God as it is being heard within that particular community, and that may therefore stifle the community's distinctive contributions to the overall life of the church.

My discussion of this ecclesiological perspective is broadly informed by my own long-term participation in parishes, as a member, in various leadership roles, and in systematic observation and study. I have developed these experiences in the Northeastern United States, several Latin American and Caribbean countries, various locations in Europe (especially northwest Germany), and Australia. In this essay, I will reference in particular a qualitative study of two parish clusters that I completed in the Archdiocese of Chicago between 2011 and 2013. These studies corroborate the central importance of several general themes that I will analyze here in three movements: rhetorical, scriptural, and practical.

A Rhetorical Argument: The Parish in Canon 515

Canon 515.1 reads in full, "A parish is a definite community of the Christian faithful established on a stable basis within a particular church; the pastoral care of the parish is entrusted to a pastor [*parochus*] as its own shepherd [*pastor*] under the authority of the diocesan bishop."[3] The first thing to notice here is that the community in question is not only stable but definite, specific. These two terms contextualize each other: a parish is neither just any fleeting collection of Christian individuals, nor a featureless abstraction. To attend to a parish properly requires coming to know the social, cultural, and spiritual circumstances of its community, as well as its institutional elements. Like any human community, the parish's stability and its specificity are in dynamic tension with each other—a situation of positive give-and-take that is built into this definition of parish. The network of relationships that make up the parish is in constant flux, as the individuals involved change and grow, flourish, diminish, move on, or die. Yet the community itself is a kind of institution in its own right, with a history, a set of connections with other communities, and a character and identity that evolve on a different timetable than those of its individual members, or of broader church institutions.

The mention of this inherent tension also brings us to the next essential part of the definition, that the parish is a certain community *of the faithful*. It belongs to the Body of Christ. With the whole church, then, its human characteristics, including its limitations, changeability, and vulnerability, are transformed by the presence of Christ's own Spirit. What might otherwise be deemed weaknesses can, in this light, be understood as aspects of the divine image that the community reflects, as places where we might encounter God, and where we might deepen our understanding of God, our theology. All of this means that the parish community's unique characteristics—its *specificity*—are set within its relationship with God, which is also the *real* source of its *stability*.

These dimensions of the reality of the parish help us to understand its *institutional* position from a different perspective. The parish, says the canon, is constituted "within a particular church," that is, this community exists *within* a diocese. It is worth noting at this point that the diocese itself is *not* specifically defined as a "community" in the Code of Canon Law, but as a "portion" of the universal church, suggesting that *smaller size*—something allowing for greater intimacy, perhaps—is being particularly valued in this canon's understanding of "community." At any rate, the connection to the larger church provided by its situation within the diocese ensures that the parish community—even as much as it is "holy ground," being a manifestation of the Body of Christ—is never to be regarded or understood *in isolation* from the larger church. The Body of Christ is inclusive of the whole church, and the parish is both constituted and enlivened by its organic link to all the faithful.

In turn, though, the link to the diocese suggests that what the parish offers—in its own particular gifts and in the specific network of relationships that shape it—is given *for the whole church*, not just for the parish's own members. That each parish "is entrusted to a pastor" who is "under the authority of the diocesan bishop" can be understood (and certainly has been seen traditionally) as providing for the protection—and control—of the parish community. More importantly, though, in our current era, this concrete, practical connection to the universal church enables the parish to accomplish an essential aspect of its proper *mission* by sharing its own Christian life with church communities beyond itself. The office of pastor is a two-directional link that helps both the parish and the diocese exercise their responsibilities toward the whole Body of Christ.

What emerges from this look at the words of the canonical definition of parish, then, is the foundation of an essential church institution. The parish is stably anchored in the faith and tradition of the universal church, and yet is missioned to contribute to that church and to the world its own particular spiritual gifts. These charisms are shaped by its own specific character, its constantly developing context, and its ongoing encounter with Christ. With this combination of solidity and dynamism, it can bring "down to earth" the astounding claims that Catholic Christians make, both about the presence and action of Christ among us and about the call to believers to be in intimate communion with him. As a constituent part of the church, linked to the whole Body of Christ, the parish community manifests the ongoing work of the Holy Spirit in many ways. It proclaims the Word, it celebrates the sacraments, and it turns into attitudes and actions its faith, hope, and love. Even as it does these things, though, it demonstrates the church's profound humanity in both its particular gifts and its inherent limitations. The parish offers believers the opportunity to encounter and grapple with the meaning of a God incarnate, whose face we are invited to see in all "these least ones" (see Matt 25:40)—the neglected, disillusioned, abused, poor, and needy not only in the wide sinful world in which the community of faith dwells, but within the community itself as well.

A Scriptural Reflection: Intimacy with Christ and the Mission of the Church

There are a number of ways to establish theological grounding for such a reading of the canonical definition of parish. Here, I will turn to some key passages from the Gospels, beginning with part of Jesus's Last Discourse in John (14:4–6, 10–12). In this passage, when the Lord tells the apostles that they already know the way to the place where he is going ahead of them, Thomas voices the fear and confusion of all the apostles: "Lord, we do not know where you are going. How can we know the way?" In response, Jesus declares himself to be "the Way, and the Truth, and the Life" (14:6). That is, this teacher whom they have come to know and depend on is himself the answer to both of Thomas's questions—neither merely the *means* to salvation, nor even simply its ultimate *aim*, but both at once.

Furthermore, Jesus declares that his words and his works come from "the Father who dwells in me" (14:10), and that "the one who believes in me will also do the works that I do" (14:12). By coming to know and follow Jesus, the earliest disciples encountered "the Way, and the Truth, and the Life" not in some abstract intellectual way, but in the intimate, relational experience that they shared with him and with one another. From the beginning, that relationship is an embodiment, a sacrament, of the Son's relationship to the Father, and is continued among us today in just that incarnate form. Lived day to day in countless ways, the meaning of this relationship is made sensible and present in the Eucharistic celebration of a stable, local community acting in communion with the whole church, that is, in a situation very much like what canon 515 calls "a parish."

If we move from these considerations of the form of our communion with the Lord and with each other and look now at a different gospel passage—Luke 10:1–12—we will see a further essential dimension of this sacred relationship. Here, as in other places in the Gospels, we see Jesus inviting his disciples—in this case, "seventy others" in addition to the Twelve—to carry this relationship outward into the world or, in other words, to share his *mission* (10:1). This sending is not just a practical "assignment," but part of the intimate friendship that he has already established with them. They will do the very work that Jesus was sent to do, using his words of peace and his deeds of healing to proclaim the reign of God (10:5–9). More than simply messengers, these disciples are sent out with responsibility and authority, and so are "apostles" even though not all are among "the Twelve." They, too, invite others to share in the work, both by praying for further "laborers [for] his harvest" (10:2) and by receiving the spiritual and material support of those whom they visit (10:7–9). The bonds of intimate, loving relationship that Jesus has created between himself and his disciples are being extended into the world as the gospel is proclaimed.

The practical, pastoral results of understanding today's parish through this scriptural lens can be read in a particularly expressive paragraph of Pope Francis's first Apostolic Exhortation, *Evangelii Gaudium*:

> *The Gospel tells us constantly to run the risk of a face-to-face encounter with others, with their physical presence which challenges us, with their pain and their pleasure, with their joy which infects us in our close and continuous interaction. True faith in the incarnate Son of God is inseparable from self-giving, from membership in the community, from service, from reconciliation with others. The Son of God, by becoming flesh, summoned us to the revolution of tenderness. (§88)*

A Practical Case: Two Parish Clusters, Two Understandings of Church

To come, at last, to the "take away" of this theological reflection for the tasks of church management, let us now consider two parish clusters in a large American archdiocese.[4]

I will refer to these clusters as "Resurrection" and "Corpus Christi." The management challenges of these parishes were, at least at first glance, remarkably similar. Each consisted of several neighboring parishes in contiguous urban neighborhoods, long associated with distinct European immigrant groups. The original communities were significantly diminished, and both clergy personnel and financial resources were in short supply, but Mass attendance was being maintained by the ongoing arrival of Latino immigrants.

At Resurrection, the departure of two pastors precipitated a process, initiated by the regional bishop, to canonically merge the three parishes in the area. This initiative came as a sudden surprise to most parishioners. A series of meetings was organized that included a few representatives of each parish, mostly lay staff and volunteers, available clergy, and archdiocesan representatives. The opportunities given for each parish to speak to the group unfolded as tense defenses by each community, over against the others, of its particular customs and prerogatives. At times, the discussions became quite rancorous. The clergy contributed explanations of their particular pastoral practices but did not feel especially empowered by the process to devise creative responses to the fears of parishioners, especially as diocesan pressure mounted to conclude the "planning" expeditiously. After a few months of occasional meetings, the bishop made an unexpected choice for the new pastor—a religious priest new to the archdiocese and to the cluster, and inexperienced in both parish and Latino ministry. A date for the official beginning of his pastorate in the new canonical parish was set, less than a year after the commencement of the original planning process. Two years later, the legal changes long since completed, this pastor was still on very uncertain ground, struggling to gain the acceptance of many parishioners. Unfinished and contentious tasks that weighed heavily on him included merging rival staffs and programs, finding uses for disused school and convent buildings in two of the former parishes, creating a broadly agreeable Mass schedule, and creating the sense of a shared community rather than three mutually suspicious subgroups.

Corpus Christi Parish had a very different merger experience. There, the process began nearly twenty years before the final achievement of a canonically merged parish. Originally, there were six separate parishes, and two processes of amalgamation took place in the early years of the overall process. Although not without trauma, these mergers were timed to anticipated departures of pastors that would have taken place in any case; existing ethnic and affinity communities (one parish had served primarily military families) were noted and respected; familiar buildings were not simply disposed of or rented out but for the most part were utilized for social services that the parishes continued to support. Pastors remained in dialogue with their congregations about all these changes as they were unfolding. After two parishes had eventually emerged from the five that entered this slow process, they arrived at an agreement with the remaining original parish (which had been untouched by the mergers up to this point) to bring their parochial grade schools together, creating a unifying project for all three existing communities.

In the meantime, quite separately from these parish processes, an outreach ministry to newly arrived immigrants in these same neighborhoods was beginning as a visiting priest formed small faith communities among them for discussion and mutual support. One of the pastors took particular interest in these groups and welcomed many Latino Catholics into his merged parish. In connection with this demographic shift, he also began to organize serious social support for new immigrants, which eventually spanned everything from English-language classes to legal assistance to provision of food, clothing, and shelter for those in need.

As these developments took place, circumstances also led to this same priest assuming the pastorates, first of the other merged parish, and then of the one remaining original parish. By that time, he had moved his first communities to a new, expansive campus purchased from an Evangelical church, and turned one of the older parish complexes over to a cooperative high school for children of low-income families. The three churches that eventually became the different worship sites of Corpus Christi Parish were this new campus (used largely by Latino Catholics), the remaining church of the other merged parish (where both Latino and Polish Catholics worship), and the large church of the one original parish (with a mixed congregation). Visits and conversations at these churches and social service agencies (in which I participated at about the same time as my observations of Resurrection Parish) demonstrated a dramatic difference between the two clusters. Unlike the situation I encountered at Resurrection, Corpus Christi had near-constant activity at all the sites. People seen at one location could easily be encountered at another, and a sense of common purpose and mission was palpable.

The Corpus Christi process could comfortably be called a "community-based" parish reorganization, even though this probably only became intentional in its latter phases. It employed transparent processes, collaborative approaches to leadership, attention to community identities, and concern for a vibrant social ministry both within and beyond the boundaries of that community. Although the process certainly did attend to some archdiocesan priorities (such as the need to address dwindling congregations and to replace departing pastors), specific initiatives and their timing were driven more by what was occurring within the communities themselves. All the difficult practical decisions had to be made, of course, regarding combining communities, closing or repurposing buildings, changing Mass schedules, adjusting staff job descriptions, and so on. Yet while all this was happening, so too was the work of listening to the communities within which parishioners lived, helping them come to understand themselves and one another more fully, assisting in the development of their lived faith, and encouraging the growth of a shared sense of mission. With all the ups and downs that surely accompanied this work, these were the characteristics that shone through in the united parish years later.

The contrast between this and the "administrative" process implemented at Resurrection is very instructive. There, the focus was almost entirely on the needs, timetable, and resources of the archdiocese. While those concerns were admittedly important and pressing in their own sphere, it was the intimate face-to-face quality of Christian community that was lost. The *specific character* of each of the parishes, and those of the neighborhoods they served, was allowed to disappear from consideration. The failure to authorize community representatives to substantively affect the outcome of the merger deliberations resulted in deep frustration. This was surely a major factor in the degeneration of that whole aspect of the planning into petty, defensive bickering that allowed easy dismissal of those parishioners and the quick conclusion of the agenda by archdiocesan officials.

They put in place the surface requirements of canon 515 with the appointment of a pastor (unqualified, by his own admission) and the setting of the date for the official creation of the new, combined community (still seriously divided years later). That this clear pastoral failure could take on the aspect of an administrative success is confirmation that the deeper implications of the canon and its theological foundations *must* be brought into focus if such decision-making is truly to build up the Body of Christ in its most local manifestations.

The other major casualty of this administrative model of parish reorganization was the genuine *mutuality* of the parish communities' relationships with the archdiocese. As we saw earlier, the relationship between the local community and wider dimensions of the universal church is based on the parish's definition as a *community of the faithful*. This faith is recognized and sustained by baptism, Eucharist, and the other sacraments, received from the whole church. But like all genuine Christian faith, it consists in the living relationship of the faithful with Christ himself. Diocesan structures, though representing the authority of the bishop, are in the service of the relationship to Christ, and to that relationship all structures and offices owe reverence. A local community, on its part, is one of a number—often a large number—of other communities under the pastoral authority of the same bishop. Their reverence is owed to the bishop as their link to the larger church, and most especially to those other communities whom the bishop serves. This network of mutual relationships, "strengthened...with power through his Spirit" and "rooted and grounded in love" as the Letter to the Ephesians prays (3:14–19), are ultimately the very substance of the church as an earthly institution. They are what the early church meant by "communion," within which Christians encounter not only one another, but Christ himself, with whom and in whom they are joined.[5] All of this means that failure to explicitly recognize and honor the local community in situations such as the Resurrection merger does damage to the very essence of the church's identity.

In the end, the potential for such damage—and its counterpoint in the potential for great flourishing—has been my primary concern in this essay. These reflections are offered as an example of the *theological discernment* that could be an ordinary part of deliberations on church management (and already is, in the best cases of which I am aware). I have presented here three different kinds of theological analysis, based on a canonical definition, a set of scripture passages, and a field experience of actual parish communities. But the heart of this theology is found not so much in arguments and scholarly sources as in practical processes that combine organizational experience and prudence with a faithful desire to understand and empower the Body of Christ here and now. It is a *discernment* process because it does not seek closed doctrinal conclusions, nor does it attempt to impose a set of sacrosanct practices beyond questioning. Rather, such theological reflection seeks the ongoing ability to recognize the gifts of the Spirit within the Christian community and to encourage their expression in an organized and sustainable way, so that the Gospel might be proclaimed and the vibrant response of those who hear it might be nurtured. Our work for the better organization and management of local Catholic parishes will be stronger and more long-lasting—and, most importantly, will further the true mission of Christ's universal church—to the degree that we are able to see, grasp, and reverence the living faith of these communities.

Notes

1.   Thomas Baima, ed., *What Is a Parish?* (Mundelein, IL: Hillenbrand, 2011) and various other works have raised the question openly in recent years, but these authors have not yet succeeded in shifting the common perception that we "ought to know that already."

2.   Francesco Coccopalmerio, "De Paroecia ut Communitate Christifidelium," *Periodica* 80 (1991): 19–44, discusses the process and reasoning by which this descriptor was included in the

1983 Code of Canon Law. (The author, a professor of canon law, eventually became a cardinal and a major figure in the Roman curia.)

3.   Canon 515.1, in James Coriden et al., eds., *The Code of Canon Law: A Text and Commentary*, Commissioned by the Canon Law Society of America (New York: Paulist Press, 1985), 415. (Terms from the original Latin have been added for clarity.)

4.   This case is considered in greater detail in William Clark, "Toward a Culture of Dynamic Community: Parish Consolidation and Collaborative Leadership," in *Collaborative Parish Leadership: Contexts, Models, Theology*, ed. Clark Gast and Dan Gast (Lanham, MD: Lexington, 2016), 75–102.

5.   Consider, e.g., this passage in "The Letter of Ignatius [of Antioch] to the Ephesians" (c. AD 110): "If in so short a time I could get so close to your bishop—I do not mean in a natural way, but a spiritual—how much more do I congratulate you on having such intimacy with him as the Church enjoys with Jesus Christ, and Jesus Christ with the Father. That is how unity and harmony come to prevail everywhere." "Letters of Ignatius: Ephesians 5:1," in Cyril C. Richardson, ed., *Early Church Fathers* (New York: Collier, 1970), 89. Note also Vatican II, "Dogmatic Constitution on the Church (*Lumen Gentium*), §51: "For if we continue to love one another and to join in praising the Most Holy Trinity—all of us who are sons of God and form one family in Christ (cf. Heb. 3:6)—we will be faithful to the deepest vocation of the Church."

2

What Do You Mean "Co-Responsible"?

Leadership in the Co-Responsible Parish

Marti R. Jewell

I invite everyone to be bold and creative in the task of rethinking the objectives, the structure, the style and the methods to evangelize communities.

—Pope Francis

They came to the Festival of Creativity, gathering with others in the *Magna Aula* of St. John Lateran University, sitting in large classrooms, enduring the difficulty of listening to translated presentations, invited to hear about research in church management. They came: Researchers, theologians, canonists, students, and parish practitioners. All were asked to think about their dream for the church in twenty years. In truth, I think they were mostly just hoping to find out how to get through day-to-day. How does anyone know what they will want in twenty years when the present is so overwhelming? Do we long for the best of the good old days? Do we settle for just getting by? Do we hope to find something new? A possibility?

The world of today's parish is changing, transforming in ways we can hardly imagine. A new story is colliding with the old. In a paradigm shift, inconceivable even fifty years ago, parish life is undergoing significant restructuring. We see changing demographics and parish personnel. Pastoral roles are evolving. Complex demands are being placed on those in ministry. These growing demands were represented in the Festival audience. In attendance was a middle-aged pastor who has fifteen thousand parishioners, sitting alongside a young new pastor who is still trying to figure out how to make everything work. Some were students of canon law studying what was still an unembodied set of rules and regulations, speaking with lay ecclesial ministers and aging women religious. What they shared is living in an era where everything is changing. Time-honored traditions, relationships, villages, all have changed. What is not changing, however, are the three major tasks parish leaders must accomplish. First, they must ensure that their parish communities are healthy, vital, and spiritually alive. Second, they must provide liturgical, sacramental, catechetical, pastoral, and social ministries. Third, they are called to animate the missionary discipleship of the baptized. In theory, these three objectives sound idyllic. Putting them into practice is another matter entirely, and attempts are often far from ideal!

Discovering how pastoral leaders accomplish the task of providing for parish life in these changing times was the objective of a nine-year research effort in the United States called *The Emerging Models of Pastoral Leadership Project* (EMP).[1] This nationwide research was tasked with finding excellence in pastoral leadership, both lay and ordained. In symposiums across the United States, participants, counterparts of others in Rome, grappled with questions of leadership and collaboration. Analysis of oral and written responses to the EMP research indicated that the ability of parish leaders to collaborate is critical to ensuring healthy parishes. Respondents demonstrated repeatedly that flourishing parishes have pastoral leaders and staffs who work well together, and where they do not, ministry appears ineffective.[2] The research also showed that pastoral leaders have different approaches to working together, and three different, broad-stroke, styles of leadership. First is the style rooted in the person of the leader who feels very responsible for the community and responsible to his or her superiors. The second focuses on working with a core team that, together with the pastor, shares in providing the programs and services for the parish. The third, and most predominant, is a leadership style in which pastor and team primarily focus on animating the community for missionary discipleship. The research also demonstrated that each of these styles has a recognizable cluster of practices, understanding of parish, and preferred ways of working with others.

As I shared these findings about how lay and ordained work together in the life of the parish at the Festival, an interesting dynamic surfaced. Each participant—pastor, parish staff person, or soon-to-be canonist—heard the findings from within their own context. The pastor of the megaparish knew that he was physically incapable of doing all the work demanded by a large parish but was concerned that if he hired pastoral staff, parishioners would stop volunteering, for him an adverse effect. The new pastor, still learning to establish his authority and trying to put his training into practice, wondered what kinds of staffing models were available to him. The canonist-in-training felt that even looking at leadership styles violated canon law. And the members of the parish staff? They shared their comments privately, unwilling to publicly discuss their frustrations. Each has a heart for ministry, but they are seemingly at odds with one another; each presenting a valid need that the church of today must meet. Whether being pragmatic or discovering a developing ecclesiology, the church is calling us to find ways in which lay and ordained can work together, co-responsible in serving the people of God. It is to this collaboration and co-responsibility that Pope Benedict XVI called the church. The laity, he said are no longer to be seen as "collaborators" in the work of the clergy, but must be truly recognized as "sharing responsibility for the existence and action of the church."[3] In what follows I will explore the three styles of leadership that surfaced in the research, and how these different styles uniquely collaborate in the mission of the parish.

The Designated Leader

Listening to the participants at the Festival, it quickly became evident that for some, the idea that persons other than the pastor could be a leader or provide leadership came as a surprise. Here, the canonists were best able to define their stance. For them, leadership belongs to the pastor and the pastor alone. At the heart of this stance, coming from a long tradition of hierarchical leadership, is canon 519, which defines the work of the pastor: "The pastor [parochus] is the proper pastor [pastor] of the parish entrusted to him, exercising pastoral care of the community committed to him under the authority of the diocesan bishop."[4] The law, they felt, is clear. A parish is assigned to a pastor, or in the absence of a pastor, to others designated by the bishop under canon 517.2.[5] As expressed by those in the room, the pastor is the leader. The leader is the one who governs. The one who governs is the one who makes decisions. In this line of thought, if only the pastor can make decisions, there can only be one kind of leadership, that is, hierarchical, and no one else can be a leader or exercise leadership.

A deeper look into the research showed that those whose understanding of leadership is rooted in the designated leader, consider the co-responsibility of others as only consultative. Canon law strongly suggests that the pastor make decisions in consultation with others. An example of this can be seen in the pastor's relationship with the parish financial and pastoral councils, which are collaborative bodies, consultative in nature.[6] In the words of one respondent to the EMP research, "Our finance council relates well with the pastor. He takes our recommendations into consideration. He has the last say, but he weighs our recommendations heavily."[7] Done well, consultative bodies can be co-responsible for the care of the health and well-being of the community. But even consulting is hard if the pastoral leader believes there is only one truth—his—and only one person he can safely rely on—himself.[8] Where consultation is done but disregarded, or not done at all, staff and parishioners experience little ownership, if not outright disregard, for their expertise and experience. Hierarchical forms are not as welcome as they once were.

As we find our way into the church of the next decade, we must stretch our understanding of leadership, how it is provided, and by whom. The term *leadership* itself is multivalent and implies more than decision-making. The prevailing understanding of the term and its practice that surfaced in the EMP research is well expressed by leadership theorists, such as Sharon Parks, as the capacity or capability to move a community through change toward its mission and vision. It is the ability to invite people to move beyond the familiar into a world of greater complexity, new learning, and new patterns of interacting.[9] Certainly, for a parish the goal is creating a healthy community that can live out the mission of the church. Given this understanding of leadership, we can see that in any parish, there will be persons in addition to the pastor designated to provide leadership in a given area, as well as "unofficial leaders" whose mere presence can provide much-needed guidance. This is well within the framework of canon 519, which speaks of the pastor as the designated leader, but also states that he is to delegate, working in cooperation with deacons and lay leaders of the community, always according to the norms of the law.[10]

In a world with a growing resistance to hierarchies,[11] the traditional model is not always welcome and can lead to low morale of otherwise capable staff, or the lack of involvement of parishioners, who will simply leave. Certainly, it can seem that it is easiest to lead by depending on oneself while meeting the many demands of parish and parishioners, especially when time and energy are in short supply. In fact, the designated leader model is the only style of leadership in the EMP research that mentioned burnout and fatigue.[12] Like Moses leading the Israelite tribes, we become weary before we reach the goal and, like Moses, we must work with others to move forward.

Leadership Shared with a Core Team

In the question about how to share leadership we begin to see the concerns of the new pastor at the Festival. He has his training, but now he needs to find a way to make it all work. Like other participants of the Festival, he was hungry for answers from those already dealing with these issues in changing contexts. How is he to staff his parish?

Many parishes still have a single, resident pastor, whom canon law presumes has a pastoral relationship with each parishioner. Yet, growing parish sizes make this nearly impossible. U.S. bishops are ordaining permanent deacons in large numbers to assist in the sacramental ministry. But to function effectively, large parishes also have lay staff who are given leadership responsibility over various areas of parish ministry. These parish teams, often called "core teams," can be small or complex, with lay pastoral ministers, permanent deacons, and parochial vicars serving alongside the pastor. Staffs often include other lay professionals for areas such as business, education, or facilities maintenance. However, the United States is not the only country with large parishes. Germany, for example, is in the process of closing or merging over half of its parishes and creating larger units. Italy is doing the same.

Other staffing models are developing alongside the growth of megachurches. Most pastors in the United States assume that they will be pastoring two or more parishes at the same time. In the course of the EMP research, we met experienced pastors as well as the newly ordained who are being given multiple parishes. Some pastors have been given multiple clusters of two or three parishes each, sometimes so far apart that they cannot maintain a single residence. Others have multiple parishes over a very large rural area, some in adjoining urban neighborhoods. Depending on size and location, there are paid staff or very involved parishioners who ensure the day-to-day operation of the parish. In parishes small and large, parishioners and staff work with the pastor in carrying out pastoral care, catechetical formation, and social outreach of the parish. So, while canon 519 does not explain how one is to provide leadership, it is evident that authorization and delegation are possible. While the pastor is always the officially designated leader, in these models we see a movement toward shared leadership, so that a core team shares in the responsibility of leadership, authorized to steward the programming, ministry, and sacramental life of the community.

Here we meet the women religious who attended the Festival. For years parishes were run by priests and sisters. This model has caught our religious imagination, perhaps because it is easy to see that women religious, along with priests, have given their lives to the church. However, especially with the increase in the average age of vowed religious, the percentage of women religious available for parish ministry is sharply declining. Women religious in the United States make up only about 14 percent of parish staffs. .

Here we encounter a second shift in parish ministry. Present also were lay ministers, both men and women, who are also giving their lives to serve the church, serving parishes that are more and more dependent on their service. In the United States there are some forty thousand lay ecclesial ministers providing parish ministry and leadership. This is more than double the number of active priests or permanent deacons, and seven times the number of women religious. These women and men, many of whom have never had an employer other than the church, showed up in the EMP studies as deeply devoted and committed to the work of the church and caring for God's people. They are living out the vision of *Lumen Gentium* 12, which calls the laity to "undertake the various tasks and offices which contribute toward the renewal and building up of the Church."

Serving as co-stewards of the community, they see themselves as co-responsible for the parish, their relationship with each other, and for the mission of the parish. The presence of lay ecclesial ministers serving in official, authorized, and designated capacities, has brought to the world of the parish an understanding of collaboration as cooperation in the dynamic of achieving a shared vision and engaging the faithful in the mission of the church, each according to their own abilities.

How to do this well is one of the biggest challenges in parish life today. The presence of lay ministers and lay professionals calls for training and formation, as Jesus gave his disciples before he sent them out in his name. When parishes move to team-based, shared leadership, pastor and staff come to appreciate that leadership is not an individual endeavor, but depends on mutual interdependence as they work together toward the same goal.[13] The successful collaboration of parish teams depends on the development of a healthy and mutual respect among the staff and with the pastor.[14] The task of the designated leader is one of developing the team, training, mentoring, and creating a shared vision for the leaders who are co-responsible for the life of the parish. From this base, each member of the team can provide leadership for that portion of parish life that has been delegated to their care. We met many lay ministers and lay professionals, men and women, as well as religious, whose fidelity in working with the pastors in serving the people of God in the face of incredible challenges is a grace to the church. Their vocation is not always recognized or welcomed, but they continue to serve. The challenge most often named by parish teams is the very human one of learning to work together: men and women, lay and ordained, supervisor and supervisee.

Pastors who value their ministry will meet this challenge to form their team, just as Jesus formed his disciples so that they could go out and do as he did.

Animating the Community

However, if we are to have a vital church in twenty years, there is a third singular and significant shift that must happen. To be the bolder, braver church to which Pope Francis is calling us,[15] we must embrace a leadership style that is focused on animating the community for mission. This goes beyond providing sacramental and pastoral care. The EMP findings show that the best, most visionary pastoral leaders see the totality, complexity, and interdependence of the entire parish. An exemplary leader is one who sees the "forest" and not just the "trees." It is critical that this person have the capacity to see the whole, whether the parish as a whole or a portion of its ministry; understand its needs and requirements; sees how the parts are interrelated; have a sense of its goal and mission and the knowledge of how to get there. Some have called this the "view from the balcony."[16] In this style the designated leader still ensures all needed decisions are made and is ultimately responsible. Together the pastor and a core team animate what the EMP called a "total ministering community."[17] To be alive and healthy in twenty years we must find ways to animate communities in which all are welcome and able to take ownership of their faith. We must recognize that our baptism calls us to adult, mature, co-responsibility in bringing the good news to the world, the mission given to all of the faithful.[18] This ideal seemed to be a challenge to current thinking about parishioners that focuses on engaging them within the parish, rather than on sending them out into the world of their daily lives. It appears that we have become so accustomed to thinking of parish as just what happens in our buildings and on our grounds that the idea of a "church without walls" in which all the baptized take leadership in spreading the good news may not be on our radar. However, if we recall that the 1983 Code of Canon Law describes the parish as being a dynamic, relational community of the faithful,[19] then we can begin to make this much-needed shift. Clearly the move toward thinking of the leadership of a parish as a community of disciples, called and sent through their baptism, co-responsible for the mission of the church, challenges us to move from a mentality of serving individual persons to engaging the total community as co-responsible for the mission. The language developed by the EMP to describe this style is "a total ministering community,"[20] recognizing the systemic nature of a community in which the actions of every person impact the whole. This is the community Benedict XVI calls "co-responsible," and we see examples of this model around the world. We find it in communities that see their pastor only occasionally because he is called to pastor multiple parishes. It is at the heart of the Diocese of Poitiers model, which has moved from parish-based to area-based ministry, engaging the community in living out the faith. Here pastors lead prayer; the community cares for one another.[21] It is the most realistic model for mega-parishes, and yet we also see it in smaller communities where the need to engage parishioners is less urgent than the desire to act as catalysts for their role in the mission of Christ.

There are challenges in this style of leadership. Both pastors and staff are called to move from thinking of the parish as an institution that serves parishioners who are volunteers, to seeing it as a community in which all have a role by virtue of their baptism. In a *communio* understanding of parish, parishioners are missionary disciples, called and sent. They are not, cannot be, "volunteers" in the community into which they have been baptized, nor is taking their faith out into the world merely an option. Pastor and staff are called to let go of being the "doers" of ministry, becoming instead "animators" of the community.

Let us return to the pastor of the mega-parish. He well recognizes that in order to ensure a vital and spiritually alive parish, parish leaders must work together to animate the community for mission. This calls today's leaders to redefine themselves with a new mindset, becoming creative and adaptive.[22] With so much shifting around them, they have the prophetic task of moving into a new paradigm, engaging the community in discernment of the invitation of the Holy Spirit and the mission of Jesus. In this movement to a total ministering parish, the designated leaders, who have a critical role in maintaining the community's vision, become catalysts for the leadership of others, calling forth their gifts and sparking new ideas. A parish business manager expressed this well, saying, "I see my role as an interpersonal role, helping to establish a welcoming environment, one that encourages leadership and empowers the community to take ownership of the parish and community life."[23]

What does this look like in practice? In many ways, though the most co-responsible model, this type of leadership is the most demanding. Here we see parishioners involved in the life of the community through such devices as "councils, committees, and commissions, all-parish meetings, town halls, and parishioner-led ministries."[24] One pastor requires every committee to ask how their decisions serve the vision of the parish before moving forward. Decision-making is built on consensus, a model preferred for important decisions by over 90 percent of parish business managers in a nationwide survey. "The process of achieving a consensus itself is healthy in that it animates participation of all, and increases the prospects for constructive controversy, involvement, cohesion, and commitment."[25] The skills needed for this model of leadership include the ability to be present and listen to the community, and calls for the development of presence-based relational skills.[26]

The unexpected challenge here, of course, is catechizing parishioners as they grow into missionary disciples. In order to continue to grow and be healthy, parishes must become *communio*, parishioners called to be adults by their baptism and sent to carry the good news, as we saw so clearly in the Pauline communities in which each one's gifts served the whole.

The Emerging Parish

Leaders and pastoral agents are called to let go of being the sole providers of ministry and open to the invitation of the Spirit coming through the community. We are discovering new styles of leadership that do not depend on extraordinary individuals,[27] but rather on those who have the capacity to cocreate the kingdom of God with open minds and open hearts. To do so, we need to "learn the disciplines that will help cultivate the wisdom of the group and larger social systems."[28] We must learn to be catalysts as the community accesses its own inner wisdom, a defining feature of our age,[29] and join our prayer with Jesus as he prays, "Father, not my will, but yours be done" (Luke 22:42). For the community there is the equally difficult challenge of letting go of being served and taking ownership of their part in the mission of the church. As we work together, we will discover that parish life is not about serving others, but about all of us responding to the divine invitation. We are in this together, a total ministering community, adults in our faith, co-responsible for the mission of Christ. Being animators of the gifts of the baptized and forming them as missionary disciples is, therefore, not a particular form of leadership. It is the demand of the gospel. We are all co-responsible for our emerging future. "I am about to do a new thing; now it springs forth, do you not perceive it?" (Isa 43:19).

Notes

1. The "Emerging Models of Pastoral Leadership Project" was a joint effort of the National Association for Lay Ministry, Conference for Pastoral Planning and Council Development, National Catholic Young Adult Ministry Association, National Association of Church Personnel Administrators,

National Association of Diaconate Directors, and Nation Federation of Priests' Councils, funded by the Lilly Endowment, Inc., in their Sustaining Pastoral Excellence Program.

2. Marti R. Jewell and David A. Ramey, *The Changing Face of Church: Emerging Models of Parish Leadership* (Chicago: Loyola Press, 2010), 78.

3. Benedict XVI, "Opening of the Pastoral Convention of the Diocese of Rome on the Theme: Church Membership and Pastoral Co-responsibility, Basilica of St. John Lateran, May 26, 2009.

4. *Code of Canon Law*, Latin-English Edition (Washington, DC: Canon Law Society of America, 1999), 519. Hereafter, CIC.

5. CIC 517.2.

6. Congregation for the Clergy et al., Instruction on Certain Questions Regarding the Collaboration of the Non-ordained Faithful in the Sacred Ministry of Priest, Article 5, no. 2., August 15, 1997, accessed March 1, 2017, https://www.vatican.va/roman_curia/congregations/cclergy/documents/rc_con_interdic_doc_15081997_en.html.

7. "The Role and Reality of Parish Business Manager and Parish Finance Council Members Report" (Washington, DC: NALM, 2012), 49.

8. C. Otto Scharmer, "2017—Trump—Are We Ready to Rise?" *Huffington Post*, December 27, 2016, accessed December 29, 2016, http://www.huffingtonpost.com/entry/5861ea62e4b014e7c72eddf2?timestamp=1482815807209.

9. See, e.g., Sharon Daloz Parks, *Leadership Can Be Taught: A Bold Approach for a Complex World* (Boston: Harvard Business School Press, 2005), 9.

10. CIC 519.

11. Andreas Henkelmann and Graciela Sonntag, "A Crisis of Trust, a Crisis of Credibility, a Crisis of Leadership: The Catholic Church in Germany in Quest of New Models," translated by Robert Schreiter in *Collaborative Parish Leadership: Contexts, Models, Theology*, ed. William A. Clark and Daniel Gast (Lanham, MD: Lexington Books, 2017), 146.

12. Marti R. Jewell, "From Practice to the Tradition and Back Again," in Clark and Gast, *Collaborative Parish Leadership*, 186.

13. Robert Kaslyn, "The Obligations and Rights of All the Christian Faithful," in *New Commentary on the Code of Canon Law*, ed. John P. Beal, James A. Coriden, and Thomas Green (New York: Paulist Press, 2000), 263.

14. Brian Froehle, "Build Collaboration, Build Church?" in Clark and Gast, *Collaborative Parish Leadership*, 63.

15. Francis, Apostolic Exhortation *Evangelium Gaudium* (The Joy of the Gospel), (2013), no. 33.

16. Ronald A. Heifitz, *Leadership without Easy Answers* (Boston: Harvard University Press, 1994), ix.

17. Jewell and Ramey, *Changing Face*, 79.

18. *Lumen Gentium* 10.

19. CIC 515.1.

20. Jewell and Ramey, *Changing Face*, 79.

21. See Richard Feiter, "The Local Communities of Poitiers: Reflections on Their Reflection," trans. Robert Schreiter, CPPS, in Clark and Gast, *Collaborative Parish Leadership*, 155–74.

22. Jewell and Ramey, *Changing Face*, vii.

23. Business Manager Report, 17.

24. Jewell and Ramey, *Changing Face*, 95.

25. "Role and Reality of Parish Business Manager," 46.

26. C. Otto Scharmer, *Theory U: Leading from the Future as It Emerges* (San Francisco: Barrett-Koehler Publishers, 2009), 75.

27. Peter Senge, C. Otto Scharmer, Joseph Jaworski, and Betty Sue Flowers, *Presence: Human Purpose and the Field of the Future* (Cambridge, MA: The Society for Organizational Learning, 2004), 191.

28. Senge et al., *Presence*, 191–92.

29. Senge et al., *Presence*, 192.

3

Parish Pastoral Leadership

The Challenge of Fostering Unity While Nurturing Diversity

Mark Mogilka

The Parish: Basics

In the training and formation of priests and parish leaders, a basic model of parish is presented. As noted in canon law, "a parish is a definite *community* of the Christian faithful established on a stable basis within a particular church; the pastoral care of the parish is entrusted to a pastor as its own shepherd under the authority of the diocesan bishop."[1] Emphasis is often placed on the importance of *community*, or maintaining unity. At the Second Vatican Council, the important image or ecclesiology of church as a community or *communio* is noteworthy.[2] St. John Paul II noted that the church is to be the "home and school of communion."[3]

The parish's purposes or reasons for existence as outlined in the *Catechism of the Catholic Church* can be summarized as:

1. To be a **community** under a pastor;

2. To be a place for the faithful to gather for **Eucharist**;

3. To be a place where Christ's saving **doctrine** is taught;

4. To be a place where **charity** is practiced.[4]

Pope Francis has added a fifth purpose, "the parish is the place that encourages and trains its members to be **evangelizers**."[5]

To help the parish to carry out its mission, a pastor is assigned by the local bishop. The pastor's role and responsibilities as outlined in canon law are "to teach, sanctify and to govern."[6] It is interesting to note the pastor's responsibility is to "govern," or as many would understand, to "manage or administer" the parish. Pope Francis has noted, "Mere administration can no longer be enough. Throughout the world let us be permanently in a state of mission."[7] Given the emerging complex and diverse models of parish, pastors need more training in administration but perhaps more importantly, formation in pastoral *leadership* of parishes.

Effective pastoral leaders articulate a vision—God's vision—and then engage people in the realization of that vision.[8] While considering the foundational purposes of the parish, one of the more challenging aspects of that vision is how much emphasis the pastor should place on fostering unity in the parish while nurturing the diverse and unique groups that comprise it. Many official church documents suggest that emphasis should be placed on fostering "unity." The primary source for this foundational vision is Jesus's prayer, "That they may all be one" (John 17:21). Some business literature tends to reinforce this value in its efforts to recommend ways to streamline organizations and create greater efficiency through standardization.

Parish Life Today: Challenges to Unity

Today, pastors and parish leaders face significant challenges in their efforts to lead parishes and foster unity. Pastors today and in the future will need to lead, not just govern or manage. Although assigned to one parish, within that parish most pastors will find not just a single community, but a community of communities. While there are many evolving changes and challenges to parish life in the U.S. church, for the purposes of this essay there are at least six noteworthy areas that challenge the vision of many pastors and lay leaders in their quest for unity.

Multiple Parish Pastoring

Initial research published in 2006 on Multiple Parish Pastoring reported that almost 50 percent of parishes, chapels, and missions in the United States shared a pastor.[9] A more recent study published in 2015 reported that 42 percent of Catholic clergy in the United States serve more than one parish.[10] According to canon law, a pastor should only serve one parish. However, "the care of several neighboring parishes can be entrusted to the same pastor due to a dearth of priests."[11] Because of a growing Catholic population and declining number of priests, this is the most common strategy employed by dioceses to respond to the challenge of fewer priests and more Catholics.

In their 2009 book, *Pastoring Multiple Parishes*, Mogilka and Wiskus outline various models and best practices for multiple parish pastoring.[12] The authors stress that there is no one way to pastor multiple parishes. Their book outlines six models for multiple parish pastoring that demonstrate varying levels of interparish cooperation and independence. All the models maintain a basic unity as seen in the symbol of the common pastor.

Pastoral leaders in multiple parish situations are also encouraged to keep in mind that each parish community they serve is a unique living organism that has a special history, may have ethnic roots, values, patterns of decision-making, rituals, traditions, and so on. In other words, each parish has a unique diverse culture that needs to be honored and respected.

Multicultural Parishes

In 2011, 38 percent of the parishes in the United States were multicultural. A multicultural parish is defined as one that has one regularly scheduled Mass each weekend in a language other than English.[13] More recent research done by CARA in 2015 reported that just under 36 percent of parishes self-identify as serving or are known to serve special racial, ethnic, or linguistic groups.[14]

To effectively lead a multicultural parish, a pastor needs to have a basic understanding of each of the unique cultures in the community. Coming to understand a culture can take years; in fact, there is not even an agreed-upon definition for *culture*. One definition is "culture primarily expresses how people live and perceive the world, one another, and God. Culture is the set of values by which a people judge, accept, and live what is considered important within the community."[15] In 2007, the U.S. Bishops established "recognition of cultural diversity" as a priority for their 2008–11 planning cycle. In 2012, the U.S. Catholic Bishops' Committee on Cultural Diversity published a book titled *Building Intercultural Competence for Ministers*.[16] The book is an excellent review and training tool to assist pastoral leaders in their efforts to acquire the "knowledge, skills, and attitudes" for intercultural competence and over time helping to understand the process for fostering unity between and among diverse cultural groups. It is interesting to note that in 2013 the same U.S. Bishops' committee published a second book titled *Best Practices for Shared Parishes*.[17] This book puts greater emphasis on nurturing diversity or ways in which cultural groups might "share" a common parish and maintain a common mission.

International Priests

The Catholic Church in the United States has always had international priests. It is only between 1940 and 1960 that North Americans produced enough homegrown priests to meet its needs. In 1985, 16 percent of the priests serving in the United States were foreign-born.[18] More recent research reports that currently 20 percent of the priests in the United States are from outside the country. One author noted that international priests bring "abundant blessings and enormous challenges." Where concerns have been reported they tend to be around language problems and cultural misunderstandings.[19] It is not uncommon for parishes in the United States to have an international priest who comes from one culture, serving parishioners who may be immigrants from still a different country, doing ministry in the culture of the U.S. Catholic parish, which operates differently than either the culture of the pastor or its parishioners.

Consolidated Parishes

In a study done in 2011, 7 percent of parishes in the United States reported that they had been "consolidated" since 2005. A consolidated parish is one that has been created through the merger or consolidation of two or more parishes.[20] Between 2000 and 2010, 725 parishes were closed. Given that most of these parishes were probably not fully closed—or suppressed, to use the canonical term—the majority were probably merged or consolidated into neighboring parishes. Therefore, it can be estimated that today about 15 percent of the parishes in the United States are consolidated. Consolidated parishes usually have one pastor, one pastoral council, one finance council, combined finances, and shared staff. In many instances, when parish communities are merged to form a new parish, their respective church buildings or sites remain open and are utilized for weekend Sunday Masses. The outward appearance of a consolidation suggests that what has been created through canonical decrees and organizational merging is a new unified parish. How-ever, pastors of consolidated parishes regularly report that within the parish they still have two or more communities of people who may cling to their past identity, experience, rituals, and traditions from their parish of origin.

In an unpublished study in the Diocese of Green Bay, Wisconsin, in 2005 there were six parishes in the same town that were within a 1.5-mile radius from the center of the city. These six were con-solidated into one canonical parish with three worship sites. In 2016, ten years after the merger of these parishes, an in-pew parish survey asked which of the following statements best describes how the merger has gone. The data is based on 1,087 returned surveys.

40%—we are 1 parish with three worship sites

17%—we are 1 parish with three communities

12%—we are 3 distinct communities that work well together

11%—we are 3 distinct communities that cooperate on some things

4%—we are 3 very separate communities

16%—I do not know/am unsure[21]

A significant number of missional initiatives fail because of cultural differences found within multiple communities served.[22] In the business world, despite the presence of employees whose livelihood or employment acts as a strong motivator to help make mergers work, there are significant challenges that must be overcome. Conversely, parishes with multiple communities are voluntary organizations. What are often seen as forced mergers can result in the loss of significant numbers of Catholics as a result.

Polarization

Polarization is defined in the *Cambridge Dictionary* as "the act of dividing something, especially something that contains different people or opinions, to divide into two completely opposing groups."[23] James Martin, SJ, has written, "Polarization is one of the gravest illnesses infecting the US Catholic Church. In fact, Catholics often have an easier time talking with members of other Christian denominations and other religious traditions than with one another. Before we can accomplish anything in our church, we must be able to talk to one another charitably."[24]

Polarization within the church is not only felt by parishioners but also among the presbyterate. This was first documented in a book published in 2012, *Same Call, Different Men* by Gauthier et al.[25] This book documented the significant divide between the generally younger "Traditionalist," sometimes referred to as cultic, priests and the generally older "Progressive," sometimes referred to as servant-leader priests. In a study done in 2009, 33 percent of priests in their sixties were rated "Progressive" while only 9 percent of those in their thirties were. On the other end of the continuum, 37 percent of priests in their thirties were considered "Traditionalists" while only 14 percent of priests in their sixties were.

Generational Differences

Numerous studies have documented the differences in church practices and beliefs between the youngest members of the faith community, Millennials, Gen-Xers, and older members, the Boomers and Elders.[26] In general, the older you are, the more likely you are to attend Mass regularly, receive the sacraments, contribute financially, and believe the basic teachings of the church. Regarding Millennials, one author noted "pastors historically mediated the transmission of knowledge to spiritual seekers but now people consult Twitter, search Google, or ask Siri."[27]

The Heart of the Challenge

Pastors and pastoral leaders who fully embrace—and perhaps are overly zealous—in fostering unity, run the risk of setting themselves up for frustration with unrealistic expectations. They also limit the potential effectiveness of their ministries through the alienation of diverse groups that make up the parish. In contrast, pastors and pastoral leaders, who in their ministerial efforts try to be all things to all the diverse groups in the parish, risk overextension, burnout, and the division of the parish with intergroup conflicts and jealousies to contend with.

To be successful, parish pastors or pastoral leaders desperately need a more balanced vision or ecclesiology of the church—one that affirms that basic unity of the parish community while affirming the unique diversity of the various groups that comprise the parish.

The Need to Clarify the Call to Foster Unity

Where tension or indifference exists among diverse groups over efforts to foster unity, it is often because of a lack of understanding of what the church teaches about the call to unity. All too often, the quest for unity (or efficiency) is translated into actions that seek uniformity. Efforts to promote uniformity do violence to the unique cultures and subgroups that constitute parish life today. An overly aggressive approach sends a message that the dominant culture is better than the subgroup or culture and thus deprives the community at large of the multitude of gifts and possibilities that a multicultural parish experience can offer.

The literature on vibrant parish life notes the critical importance of a community that practices hospitality.[28] A poorly formed understanding of the call to unity can result in the alienation of various "different" cultural groups and the failure of the parish community to live the value of "All Are Welcome." As Pope Francis noted,

> Unity does not imply uniformity; it does not necessarily mean doing everything together or thinking in the same way. Nor does it signify a loss of identity. Unity in diversity is the opposite: it involves the joyful recognition and acceptance of the various gifts which the Holy Spirit gives to each one and the placing of those gifts at the service of all members of the Church. It means knowing how to listen, to accept differences and having the freedom to think differently and express oneself with complete respect towards the other who is my sister and brother. Do not be afraid of differences.[29]

While I believe that the dominant ecclesiology in the Catholic Church calls us to unity, there is another, equally valid, scripturally based ecclesiology. That is the image of the church as the Body of Christ. This image comes directly from the Second Vatican Council's document *Lumen Gentium*.[30] As Pope Francis noted in 2013, the church is first a "living body that walks and acts in history. And this body has a head, Jesus, who guides, feeds and supports it." The Holy Father went on to note that "as members of the human body, although different and many, we form one body, as we were all baptized by one Spirit into one body (cf. 1 Cor 12:12–13). In the church, therefore, there is a variety, a diversity of tasks and functions; there is no dull uniformity, but the richness of gifts that the Holy Spirit distributes."[31] More recently the Holy Father noted, "We would not do justice to the logic of the incarnation if we thought of Christianity as monocultural and monotonous."[32]

St. Paul's letter to the Ephesians notes,

> Be completely humble and gentle; be patient, bearing with one another in love. Make every effort to keep the unity of the Spirit through the bond of peace. There is one body and one Spirit..., speaking the truth in love we will grow to become in every respect the mature body of him who is the head, that is, Christ. From him the whole body, joined and held together by every supporting ligament, grows and builds itself up in love as each part does its work. (Eph 4:1–7, 11–16; NIV)

This passage of scripture outlines many of the key values for the Body of Christ image of church. Those values include a parish that is "humble, and gentle; patient, bearing with one another in love," nurtures the one Spirit of God through a bond of mutual respect for the diverse parts of the body in peace as each unique and diverse part of the body does its special work.

The reality of parish life now and into the future is so much more than the homogeneous model of parish that is often held up as an ideal. As previously noted, parishes are richly diverse and complex. "The parish is not an outdated institution; precisely because it possesses great flexibility, it can assume quite different contours depending on the openness and missionary creativity of the pastor and the community."[33] To be vibrant and alive, parishes need a vision of church based on the image of the Body of Christ that affirms unity but also holds up more strongly the value of flexibility and diversity.

What Needs to Be Done?

Address the Fears

Address the anxiety reported by priests who serve multiple communities.[34] One must ask whether such anxiety leads to a self-fulfilling prophecy. "Nobody can go off to battle unless he is fully convinced of the victory beforehand. If we start without confidence, we have already lost half the battle," says Pope Francis.[35] The research shows that overall, priests in the United States are happy,[36] and that includes those who serve multiple parishes.[37] Parishioners do not think any less of pastors who are shared with another community than those who serve a single community.[38] Change from a more static model of parish to one that is more flexible and diverse can be unsettling for many in the church. As Pope Francis has noted, however, we must "abandon the complacent attitude that says—We have always done it this way."[39]

Update Training and Formation

Historically, seminaries have done a good job of providing formation and training for young men to be priests. Following ordination, new priests were often assigned to larger, homogeneous parishes with multiple parish staff members. These assignments served as a kind of apprenticeship program, and over the course of a few years, the newly ordained learned how to be priests and eventually pastors.

Today, due to clergy shortages, in most dioceses the time between ordination and appointment as a pastor has been reduced to only a few years. Many have not yet learned how to be good priests, much less acquire the skills for governance, administration, or pastoral leadership. Furthermore, first assignments as pastors tend to be to smaller parishes or multiple small parishes that have few if any staff. The result has been higher levels of stress and feelings of being overworked and overwhelmed, as reported by younger priests.[40]

Two recommendations are offered:

1. Initial assignments of newly ordained should be to either multicultural or multiple parish situations so that the newly ordained can learn the challenges and opportunities that such parish pastoral leadership situations provide.

2. Dioceses need to establish mandatory new-pastor programs that provide support groups and training in pastoral administration and adaptive leadership. The curriculum should also have a significant component in the areas of multiple parish pastoring, cultural intelligence (CQ),[41] and intercultural competence, as well as how to be a pastoral leader during times of change and transition such as the closing, consolidation, rebuilding, and revitalizing of parishes.[42]

It should be noted that this program should be open to and would also be a significant help to international priests serving parishes in the United States.

Business Management Training

It should be noted from the outset here that when recommending business management training it is important to recognize the truth that the church is more than a business. However, as noted in Paul's letter to the Romans 12:6–8, we find that one of the gifts of the Holy Spirit is the gift of administration. While the church is not run solely as a business, there are many tools that can be learned and used by pastors and pastoral leaders that can increase the effectiveness of complex parish systems and can assist the parish in its efforts to carry out the mission of the church.

Among the various areas that may be covered in a business curriculum for pastors and pastoral leaders might be the following:

- Management basics: setting priorities, pastoral strategic planning, making decisions, running meetings, time management, basic facility maintenance and management outsourcing, soliciting parishioner feedback, marketing
- Basic accounting: fiscal systems, budgeting, internal controls, fundraising
- Personnel management: how to recruit, interview, hire, mentor, supervise, delegate and not abdicate responsibilities, annual reviews, progressive discipline, terminations, benefits management[43]

Pastoral Leadership Training

We must move beyond the idea from canon law of a pastor's role being to "govern" a parish. There are many ways to interpret what it means to "govern." However, the dominant image is of a top-down authoritarian model of management. Social science and business literature have noted that there are some contexts in which such a model is helpful and even needed. However, in general, this model has limited utility in today's vibrant, diverse, Catholic community.

The church needs better training in leadership. *Leadership* can be defined as "the ability to articulate a vision and get others to carry it out."[44] This is a good place to begin an exploration of the topic. However, the church desperately needs *pastoral* leaders. Pastoral leaders are collaborative servant leaders who know how to engage the whole community in reflection on the rich traditions of our church and then facilitate a process of discerning the will of God or groaning of the Spirit for the common good of the community as it plans for the future. There are several excellent resources that could be part of a formation program for pastors and parish leaders.[45]

Hire or Mentor Leaders

Pastors of wisdom and experience who have served multiparish and multicultural communities know that they can't do it alone. They need help. They know how to find it and know how to delegate, not abdicate, responsibility to those helpers. In the best situations, they will hire trained and formed people. In less than ideal circumstances, they just find people who are willing. As Pope Benedict XVI has noted, "I think it is very important to find the right ways to delegate..., [the priest] should be the one who holds the essential reins himself, but he can rely on collaborators."[46]

In the United States today, there are more permanent deacons than there are parishes—17,233 parishes and 18,173 deacons. In addition, there are 39,651 lay ecclesial ministers.[47] Many of these ministers are underutilized in their parish communities.

In 1999, St. John Paul II wrote, "A renewed parish needs the collaboration of lay people and therefore a director of pastoral activity and a pastor who is able to work with others."[48] At present,

28 percent of parishes in the United States employ a business manager.[49] Cross-denominational research in the United States notes that Protestant pastors spend 14 percent of their time administering their congregations and attending meetings while Catholic pastors spend 31 percent of their time administering their parishes.[50] In 2007, while meeting with a group of Italian priests, Pope Benedict noted that pastors of multiple parishes needed "to be pastors and not become a holy bureaucrats."[51] The parishes of today and tomorrow need to take a good hard look at whether they are being good stewards of the many ministerial gifts priests bring to the parish and consider making some changes.

Nurturing Diversity

Learn Adaptive Leadership

Adaptive leadership is a leadership framework that helps priests and pastoral leaders adapt and thrive in challenging environments.[52] For parish leaders serving diverse communities and cultures, the ability to adapt to constantly changing and challenging situations is critical. A one-size-fits-all approach to leadership has been well documented as a formula for failure.

The adaptive nature of leadership and the flexibility of the parish has been noted by Pope Francis: "The parish is not an outdated institution; precisely because it possesses great flexibility, it can assume quite different contours depending on the openness and missionary creativity of the pastor and the community."[53]

Adaptive leadership has been part of the church since the beginning. St. Paul was an adaptive leader. As he noted in his first letter to the Corinthians:

> For though I am free with respect to all, I have made myself a slave to all, so that I might win more of them. To the Jews I became as a Jew, in order to win Jews. To those under the law I became as one under the law (though I myself am not under the law) so that I might win those under the law. To those outside the law I became as one outside the law (though I am not free from God's law but am under Christ's law) so that I might win those outside the law. To the weak I became weak, so that I might win the weak. I have become all things to all people, that I might by all means save some. (1 Cor 9:19–22)

See Parish as Community of Communities

St. John Paul II noted that "there is a need to keep looking for ways in which the parish and its pastoral structures can be more effective and efficient....One way of renewing parishes might be to consider the parish as a community of communities and movements."[54] Pope Francis has also noted, "In the church, variety, which is always grounded in the harmony of unity is like a great mosaic."[55] The image is a good one. It balances the importance of each unique diverse piece of the mosaic while together creating a singular, unified, larger, beautiful picture or work of art.

Lead with Cultural Competence

Given the growing diversity of communities that pastors and parish leaders of today and tomorrow serve, training in "Cultural Intelligence"[56] should be foundational. In addition to the already-mentioned publications of the U.S. Bishops Committee on Cultural Diversity, the work of Eric Law is recommended. Law uses the image of an iceberg to help pastoral leaders to understand the external and perhaps more important internal aspects of diverse cultures. He notes that many in leadership make the mistake of thinking they can bring diverse groups together by focusing on or changing the externals—the 15 percent of the iceberg above the water—those things that you can see, touch, taste, and feel. As noted by Law, if there is resistance and conflict between cultural groups, it is probably because the leaders failed to consider the 85 percent of the iceberg below the water. It is here that you find the often-unconscious important matters of the heart and soul such as a group's values, attitudes, traditions, and will. When the matters of the heart and soul are named, honored, and respected, the possibilities for cooperation and collaboration grow significantly.[57]

Do Cultural Exegesis and Compatibility Assessments

Many pastors and parish leaders who serve diverse communities are frustrated in their attempts to get the various communities to cooperate or collaborate (think foster unity) in a timely manner. This is often due to their unrealistic expectations concerning the compatibility or abilities of the cultures they serve. To help leaders to create a more realistic set of expectations, and thereby lower their levels of frustration, I often recommend that they do an assessment or cultural exegesis to determine the cultural compatibility of the cultures involved. Such an assessment requires the leader to work with representatives of the respective groups to consider such things as their history, ethnic roots, rituals and traditions, economic status, geography, and so on. Cultures that have a greater level of compatibility have a greater likelihood of building community together over a shorter period of time. Cultures with lower levels of compatibility will take much longer before they can truly cooperate and collaborate with one another. In some instances, this coming together may take generations.

In some instances, cultural incompatibly may be so strong that the best approach may be to have a "shared parish." A "shared parish" has a single church facility shared by distinct cultural groups that retain their own worship and ministries. The fastest growing and most common of these are Catholic parishes shared by Latino and white Catholics.[58] In 2000, 22 percent of the parishes in the United States met this definition. By 2015, this number had grown to 33 percent.[59] Patience and discernment are key tools needed by pastoral leaders as they explore the possibilities for intercultural cooperation and collaboration.

Fostering Unity

Cross-Cultural Trust and Relationships

When serving diverse parish or cultural communities, pastors and parish leaders must cultivate their intercultural competence, which is the capacity to communicate, relate, and work across cultural boundaries.[60] Successful pastors of multiparish and multicultural communities learn to love and serve people where they are and not try to force a false sense of unity or community. Pope Francis notes, "When leaders in various fields ask me for advice, my response is always the same: dialogue, dialogue, dialogue."[61] Pope Francis has often talked about the importance of developing the "art of accompaniment…that teaches us to remove our sandals before the sacred ground of the other."[62]

Interaction

To help facilitate the trust, understanding, respect, and relationships that can help diverse communities to cooperate and collaborate with one another, more than simple social events are needed.

In parish contexts, this includes such things as intercultural or interparish weekend retreats, small group Bible study, and prayer experiences. The Diocese of Green Bay, Wisconsin, has developed a model that uses parish leadership summits where parish leaders from diverse groups gather for a Friday evening and Saturday morning to share their hopes and dreams for the parish, brainstorm ways to help the parish to grow, set priorities, and then brainstorm actions steps. Using an Ignatian model of discernment for diverse group decision-making can also be helpful.[63]

Some of the best tools available from the business world for fostering creative problem-solving, planning, and shared action of diverse groups include the planning processes known as Appreciative Inquiry, World Café, and Open Space.[64] Each of these tools provides diverse groups of people with an opportunity to unlock their pastoral imaginations, "think outside the box," and create new possibilities for the church.

Insights from Social Psychology

In our attempts to foster unity between diverse groups, study of the insights from the field of social psychology, especially from a classic study known as the Robbers Cave Experiment, can be helpful.[65] To summarize, researchers organized boys at a summer camp who interacted well with one another into separate groups. They helped them to create strong bonds, group relationships, and a unique identity. They then put the groups into competition with one another. The result was disunity in the camp and violence among the groups. The researchers tried to undo the animosity and social barriers among the groups by disbanding them and holding socials. The groups resisted the "attack" on their groups and did not mix with people from the "other" groups. The more the researches called attention to the need for unity, the more the boys resisted.

After several failed attempts to rebuild overall camp spirit, the researches backed away from the goal of fostering unity. Instead, what they came up with was a series of work projects that could only be accomplished by the diverse teams working together. During their time working together, they reestablished relationships. The boys created a new identity built on the pride of accomplishment of the tasks put before them. When it was time to leave camp, the boys got on the bus and freely interacted with one another, regardless of their original group identity. By making task accomplishment the goal, the subordinate goal of creating an overall camp spirit or unity was accomplished.

For diverse groups in a parish, the lesson might be don't try to break down the walls among groups by stating this as your goal. Instead, help diverse groups to work together. By working together and accomplishing something, new relationships are formed, new group identity emerges, and over time, unity can be achieved. To find fun, fresh, creative projects for diverse groups to work on together and foster greater unity in the parish, do an internet search for "Random Acts of Kindness." As noted on one of the websites, doing random acts of kindness is evangelization through kindness.

Branding

Branding is the practice of creating a name, symbol, or design that identifies and differentiates a product from other products. One author noted that "having an effective brand gives you a major edge in increasingly competitive markets."[66] In the religious marketplace in which the Catholic church competes today, could the development and promotion of a common "brand" be a helpful tool to foster a greater sense of unity? How might a clear identifiable brand help with the call to evangelization to help differentiate what makes us Catholics unique and more interesting? How many times have you driven through a town and wondered, Is that church a Catholic Church? Without an easily identifiable brand, logo, or insignia it is hard to determine.

Additional Areas for Study

Multisite Churches

This is an exploding field within Protestant communities in the United States. Instead of building bigger megachurches, a new trend within Protestant communities is the establishment of multisite communities. A multisite community is defined as one that "shares a common vision, budget, leadership and board."[67] One of the advantages of multisite churches are that they have low overhead costs. They do this by going out into neighborhoods, renting space, and holding services in theatres, schools, community centers, assisted living facilities, and the like. Each site or campus has a local leader, good music, and often the message or sermon comes from the main church and is projected on a screen.[68] In 1990 there were 10 multisite communities in the United States. By 1998, there were 100; by 2005, the phenomena had grown to 1,500; and in 2014, according to research done by the Leadership Network, there were 8,000.[69] Research notes that 10 percent of all Sunday churchgoers in the United States worship in multisite congregations.[70] Pope Francis has challenged the church to go out and be a "field hospital."[71] In what the Pew Research group calls the "competitive religious marketplace," can we as a Catholic community in North America not take notice and see what we can learn from this approach?

Use of Virtual Office/Meeting Space and Technology

Among Protestant communities in North America there has been an explosion of creative applications of technology in various ministries of administration, communications, building and extending community, making and nurturing disciples, online communities, and so on. Go to the internet and type into your search engine "ChMS Church Management Software," "church software," "church technology," "internet church," or "church social media." For more inspiration as to the power and possibilities for creative use of the digital world, search for either "Catholic" or "church" in the Apple or Android app stores.

Another area for consideration, especially when there are multiple parishes and long distances between the communities served, is the development of technology systems that provide virtual office spaces, online meetings, distance learning, Bible studies, and internet communities. Many of these only require a smartphone, software, or an app. Most pastors are not ready for the internet or social media to be the only medium for connectivity, spiritual or religious experience. Their physical presence in the gathered community, in prayer and service, is still important, yet they do acknowledge that technology has become and will continue to be an especially important tool for connection, outreach, and even spiritual formation.[72]

Resistance to the use of technology or "technophobia" is not unique to the Catholic community. However, when pastors and parish leaders are trying to organize and maintain relationships among diverse communities, some of these new tools can be a major help. Better training of priests, parish leaders, and parishioners to overcome this stumbling block will be critical if the church is going to make use of these new tools for ministry. Younger generations are already using them daily in their personal and work lives. More than half of Millennials begin and end each day by checking their phones.[73]

A partial list of some to the technology tools available to assist the mission of the church includes the following:

- Accounting systems (especially for payroll)
- Volunteer management
- Virtual staff meetings

- Common calendar
- Digital communication and presence for extending community
- Individual parish community apps
- Use of social media for evangelization

Franchising

Businesses that regularly deal with the challenge of maintaining unity while respecting diversity are those that franchise their operations. To be successful, franchise operations must maintain a delicate balance between the franchisor and the franchisee. The church can learn from these how diocesan offices (franchisors) might serve parishes and or multiple community parish systems (franchisees). There is a considerable body of literature outlining best practices, technology tools, phases of franchisee training, ways to maintain brand standards and loyalties, guidelines for maintaining the corporate culture, audit support systems, and so on, that may provide some new creative insights.

Conclusion

This paper began with a quick review of the basic and foundational understanding of parish as found in canon law and the *Catechism of the Catholic Church*. It was suggested that the dominant ecclesiology or vision for the parish is unity. Six challenges to the vision of unity were offered including the growing incidence of multiparish pastoring, multicultural parishes, the growing number of international priests, consolidated parishes, polarization, and generational differences. It was suggested that the call to unity may not be a realistic vision or ecclesiology for the parish now or in the future. To continue holding up the ideal of unity can frustrate pastoral leaders and alienate diverse cultural groups.

Instead, it was recommended that a better vision or ecclesiology for the parish is the understanding of the parish as the Body of Christ. The Body of Christ image of the church provides a better response to the challenge of fostering unity, with Christ as the head, while nurturing diversity with respect for how each member's important role and each unique cultural group that makes up the parish contributes to the whole. A variety of practical and creative suggestions were offered on how the church can foster unity while nurturing diversity.

The ministerial challenges are considerable. However, if we truly believe that "nothing is impossible with God" and trust in the power and presence of the Holy Spirit, then all our challenges will be transformed into opportunities for virtuous action, and together we will see the reign of God become more and more a reality in our world.

Notes

1. James A. Coriden, Thomas J. Green, Donald E Heintschel, eds., *The Code of Canon Law: A Text and Commentary* (New York: Paulist Press, 1985), can. 515.

2. Vatican Council II, *Lumen Gentium* (November 21, 1964), http://www.vatican.va/archive/hist_councils/ii_vatican_council/documents/vat-ii_const_19641121_lumen-gentium_en.html.

3. John Paul II, Apostolic Letter *Novo Millennio Ineunte* (January 6, 2001), no. 43, http://www.vatican.va/content/john-paul-ii/en/apost_letters/2001/documents/hf_jp-ii_apl_20010106_novo-millennio-ineunte.html.

4. *Catechism of the Catholic Church* (New York: Doubleday, 1994), no. 2179.

5. Francis, Apostolic Exhortation *Evangelii Gaudium*—The Joy of the Gospel (November 24, 2013), no. 28, http://www.vatican.va/content/francesco/en/apost_exhortations/documents/papa-francesco_esortazione-ap_20131124_evangelii-gaudium.html.

6. Coriden, Green, and Heintschel, *Code of Canon Law*, can. 519.

7. Francis, *Evangelii Gaudium*, no. 25.

8. Jeffrey A. Krames, *Lead with Humility: 12 Leadership Lessons from Pope Francis* (New York: American Management Association, 2015), xiii.

9. Katarina Schuth, *Priestly Ministry in Multiple Parishes* (Collegeville, MN: Liturgical Press, 2006), 21.

10. Mark Chaves, *Religious Congregations in 21st Century America: National Congregations Study* (2015), see www.soc.duke.edu/natcong.

11. Coriden, Green, Heintschel, *Code of Canon Law*, can. 526.

12. Mark Mogilka and Kate Wiskus, *Pastoring Multiple Parishes* (Chicago, IL: Loyola Press, 2009), 83–100, 111–36.

13. Mark M. Gray, Mary L. Gautier, Melissa A. Cidade, "The Changing Face of U.S. Catholic Parishes," in *Emerging Models of Pastoral Leadership* (Washington, DC: National Association for Lay Ministry, 2011), 11.

14. Charles E. Zech, Mary L. Gautier, Mark M. Gray, Jonathon L. Wiggins, Thomas P. Gaunt, *Catholic Parishes of the 21st Century* (New York: Oxford University Press, 2017), 109.

15. National Conference of Catholic Bishops, *National Plan for Hispanic Ministry* (Washington, DC: USCCB, 1988), cited in *Building Intercultural Competence for Ministers*, 8.

16. United States Conference of Catholic Bishops, *Building Intercultural Competence for Ministers* (Washington, DC: USCCB, 2012).

17. United States Conference of Catholic Bishops, *Best Practices for Shared Parishes* (Washington, DC: USCCB, 2013).

18. Dean R. Hoge and Aniedi Okure, *International Priests in America* (Collegeville, MN: Liturgical Press, 2006), 5–6.

19. Mary L. Gautier, Paul M. Perl, Stephen J. Fichter, eds., *Same Call, Different Men* (Collegeville, MN: Liturgical Press, 2012), 77, 84.

20. Mark, Gautier, and Cidade, "Changing Face of U.S. Catholic Parishes," 11.

21. Diocese of Green Bay Wisconsin, Department of Stewardship & Pastoral Services, "St. Francis of Assisi Manitowoc Parishioner Survey Results," 2016.

22. David A. Livermore, *Cultural Intelligence* (Grand Rapids, MI: Baker Academic, 2009), 12.

23. *Cambridge Dictionary*, s.v. "polarization," accessed October 2, 2020, https://dictionary.cambridge.org/us/dictionary/english/polarization.

24. Mary Ellen Konieczny, Charles C. Camosy, Tricia C. Bruce, eds., *Polarization in the US Catholic Church* (Collegeville, MN: Liturgical Press, 2016), preface.

25. Gautier, Perl, and Fichter, *Same Call, Different Men*, 74, 87.

26. Christian Smith, Kyle C. Longest, Jonathan Hill, and Kari Marie Christoffersen, *Young Catholic America: Emerging Adults in, Out of, and Gone from the Church* (New York: Oxford University Press, 2014), 34–52; Zech et al., *Catholic Parishes of the 21st Century*, 105–6, 142; William V. D'Antonio, James D. Davidson, Dean R. Hoge, and Mary L. Gautier, *American Catholics Today: New Realities of Their Faith and Their Church* (Lanham, MD: Sheed & Ward, 2007), 39–41.

27. Barna Group, *Barna Trends 2017: What's New and What's Next at the Intersection of Faith and Culture* (Grand Rapids: Baker Books, 2016), 204.

28. James Mallon, *Divine Renovation* (New London, CT: Twenty-Third Publications, 2014); William E. Simon, *Great Parishes* (Notre Dame, IN: Ave Maria Press, 2016), 94, 101, 105, 140.

29. Francis, Address to Members of the Catholic Fraternity of Charismatic Covenant Communities and Fellowships, October 31, 2014, http://www.vatican.va/content/francesco/en/speeches/2014/october/documents/papa-francesco_20141031_catholic-fraternity.html.

30. Second Vatican Council, *Lumen Gentium* (November 21, 1964), http://www.vatican.va/archive/hist_councils/ii_vatican_council/documents/vat-ii_const_19641121_lumen-gentium_en.html.

31. Francis, Address to Members of the Catholic Fraternity of Charismatic Covenant Communities.

32. Francis, *Evangelii Gaudium*, no. 117.

33. Francis, *Evangelii Gaudium*, no. 28.

34. Jeff Rexhausen, Michael Cieslak, Mary Gautier, and Robert J. Miller, *A National Study of Recent Diocesan Efforts as Parish Reorganization in the United States* (Published by the Conference for Pastoral Planning and Council Development, 2003), 31–32.

35. Francis, *Evangelii Gaudium*, no. 85.

36. Stephen J. Rossetti, *Why Priests Are Happy* (Notre Dame, IN: Ave Maria Press, 2011), 83.

37. Schuth, *Priestly Ministry in Multiple Parishes*, 83.

38. Mark M. Gray, *Special Report: Multi-parish Ministry Findings: Emerging Models of Pastoral Leadership* (Washington, DC: National Association for Lay Ministry, 2012), 43.

39. Francis, *Evangelii Gaudium*, no. 23.

40. Rossetti, *Why Priests Are Happy*, 9.

41. David A. Livermore, *Leading with Cultural Intelligence* (New York: American Management Association, 2015), 3.

42. Charles E. Zech and Robert J. Miller, *Listening to the People of God: Closing, Rebuilding, and Revitalizing Parishes* (Mahwah, NJ: Paulist Press, 2008), 17–20.

43. Paul A. Holmes, ed., *A Pastor's Toolbox* (Collegeville, MN: Liturgical Press, 2014), 1–3; Smith & Wright, *The Church Leader's MBA* (Circleville, OH: OCU Press, 2011), 5–10, 179–90.

44. Jeffrey A. Krames, *Lead with Humility: 12 Leadership Lessons from Pope Francis* (New York: American Management Association, 2015), xiii.

45. Ann M. Garrido, *Redeeming Administration: 12 Spiritual Habits for Catholic Leaders in Parishes, Schools, Religious Communities, and Other Institutions* (Notre Dame, IN: Ave Maria Press, 2013), 4–11; Donald Senior, *The Gift of Administration* (Collegeville, MN: Liturgical Press, 2016), 23–42; Owen Phelps, *Leading Like Jesus* (Huntington, IN: Our Sunday Visitor, 2009), 17–21.

46. Benedict XVI, Meeting with the Clergy of the Dioceses of Belluno-Feltre and Treviso, July 24, 2007, http://www.vatican.va/content/benedict-xvi/en/speeches/2007/july/documents/hf_ben-xvi_spe_20070724_clero-cadore.html.

47. CARA. Center for Applied Research in the Apostolate at Georgetown University, Washington, DC. Basic data downloaded May 2017, https://cara.georgetown.edu/frequently-requested-church-statistics/.

48. John Paull II, *The Church in America: Ecclesia in America* (Washington, DC: United States Catholic Conference, 1999), 71.

49. Zech et al., *Catholic Parishes of the 21st Century*, 62.

50. Jackson W. Carroll, *God's Potters: Pastoral Leadership and the Shaping of Congregations* (Grand Rapids: William B. Eerdmans Publishing, 2006), 107.

51. Benedict XVI, Meeting with Clergy, *Origins* 37, no. 12 (August 30, 2007).

52. Ronald Heifetz, Alexander Grashow, Marty Linsky, *The Practice of Adaptive Leadership* (Boston: Harvard Business Press, 2009), 14–17.

53. Francis, *Evangelii Gaudium*, no. 28.

54. John Paull II, *Church in America*, no. 70.

55. Francis, *Evangelii Gaudium*, no. 28.

56. David A. Livermore, *Cultural Intelligence* (Grand Rapids: Baker Academic, 2009), 13.

57. Eric H. Law, *Sacred Acts, Holy Change: Faithful Diversity and Practical Transformation* (St. Louis: Chalice Press, 2002), 36–45.

58. Brett C. Hoover, *The Shared Parish: Latinos, Anglos, and the Future of U.S. Catholicism* (New York: New York University Press, 2014), 2.

59. Hoover, *Shared Parish*, 181.

60. USCCB, *Building Interpersonal Competence for Ministers* (2012), 9.

61. Francis, Meeting with Brazil's Leaders of Society, Apostolic Journey to Rio de Janeiro on the Occasion of XXVIII World Youth Day, July 27, 2013, http://www.vatican.va/content/francesco/en/speeches/2013/july/documents/papa-francesco_20130727_gmg-classe-dirigente-rio.html.

62. Francis, *Evangelii Gaudium*, no. 169.

63. James Martin, *The Jesuit Guide to Almost Everything* (New York: Harper Collins, 2010), 305–38.

64. David L. Cooperrider, Diana Whitney, Jacqueline M. Stavros, *Essentials of Appreciative Inquiry* (Brunswick, OH: Crown Custom Publishing, 2008), 3–26; Juanita Brown, *The World Café* (San Francisco: Berrett-Koehler Publishers, 2005), 12–25; Harrison Owen, *Open Space Technology: A User's Guide* (San Francisco: Berrett-Koehler Publishers, 2008), 79–106.

65. Muzafer Sherif, O. J. Harvey, William R. Hood, Carolyn W. Sherif, and Jack White, *Intergroup Conflict and Cooperation: The Robbers Cave Experiment*, cited on the website Classics in the History of Psychology, 1954/1961, http://psychclassics.yorku.ca/Sherif/.

66. *Small Business Encyclopedia*, s.v. "branding," accessed October 2, 2020, https://www.entrepreneur.com/encyclopedia.

67. Geof Surratt, Greg Ligon, and Warren Bird, *The Multi-Site Church Revolution* (Grand Rapids: Zondervan, 2006), 18.

68. Surratt, Ligon, and Bird, *Multi-Site Church Road Trip*, 148–57.

69. Warren Bird, *5 Trends in How Multisite Churches Start and Grow*, Leadership Network, www.leadnet.org, posted February 19, 2014.

70. Mark Chaves, "Religious Congregations in 21st Century America," National Congregations Study (2015), www.soc.duke.edu/natcong.

71. Antonio Spadaro, "A Big Heart Open to God: An Interview with Pope Francis," *America*, September 30, 2013, https://www.americamagazine.org/faith/2013/09/30/big-heart-open-god-interview-pope-francis.

72. *Barna Trends 2017*, 171.

73. *Barna Trends 2017*, 81.

4

The Entrepreneurial Spirit in a Mission-Driven Church

Administration for a Pastoral Future

Christian Olding, Thomas de Nocker, and Maximilian Warmbrunn

Introduction

The German Catholic Church is changing. Believers have been leaving the church, the number of baptisms has been dropping dramatically, and dioceses are desperately looking for young priests. In 2016, about 162,000 Catholics left the church. Today only about 55 percent of Germans are Christians, compared to more than 90 percent sixty years ago. Many of them do not regularly attend services. Thus, the German Catholic Church is in crisis. Only if it has a solid and authentic pastoral concept and team, will the church be able to stop this outflow and consolidate the status quo. Pope Francis himself proposed some impulses for this pastoral change: "I prefer a Church which is bruised, hurting and dirty because it has been out on the streets, rather than a Church which is unhealthy from being confined and from clinging to its own security" (EG 49). The church should take the initiative and proactively go to the edges of society, to the poor, and should enter a dialogue with the modern world. Dioceses must consider specific contexts and pastoral teams to adjust to the respective situations. In a world of globalization, digitalization, and demographic change, new ways of evangelization must be found.

To tackle this pastoral challenge, pastoral teams, priests, pastors, and volunteers need functioning administrative support in the background. By being a good working engine, administration is the basis of the proclamation of the gospel. Through various institutions the German Catholic Church is actively present in society and can validate the ongoing and life-giving gift of the gospel. These institutions include, for example, daycare centers, kindergartens, schools, and counseling facilities for marriages, families, or people in debt. To enable these different areas of pastoral work to support the kingdom of God, the church needs efficient administration. Thus, administration is an important link between the gospel and effective pastoral work. All twenty-seven German dioceses have a general vicarage with responsibilities for parishes, schools, and general administration as their main administrative body to coordinate and organize their work. Up to seven hundred people work in the general vicarages of the larger German dioceses.

The general vicarage is also responsible for redistributing the funds from church taxes. In contrast to many other countries, the German Catholic and Protestant Churches are dependent on church taxes rather than donations. Every member of the institutional churches pays up to an additional 8 or 9 percent (depending on their province) of their income tax to the church. The German state is responsible for collecting that money and gets compensation for this service. The church tax makes up around 80 percent of the budget of a diocese and gave up to 6.15 billion Euros for the whole German Catholic Church in 2016. The general vicarages then are responsible for redistributing the money to their parishes. The head of the general vicarage is the vicar general, who is appointed by the bishop of a diocese. Every diocese is split into multiple parishes managed by priests that are partly independent of the general vicarage.

Because pastoral work is undergoing a great deal of change, the general vicarage must change as well. The church cannot afford to have a static and inefficient administration, leading to deficits in pastoral work. Often, general vicarages are self-referential and turned toward inward problems rather than on needed services. This leads to blindness toward upcoming problems and to the creation of services no one wants or needs.

But what kind of administration, what kind of vicarage, does pastoral work need in the future? How can a vicarage and the whole diocesan administration be organized to support the parishes and the other pastoral entities in the best way possible? The general vicarage is not just an office, it is a pastoral enabler, and thus needs pastoral reflection. A pastor working for the church expects such an administrative structure. According to these expectations, the general vicarage must develop on many levels: service, control and transparency, and professional completion of administrative tasks. Finally, the general vicarage also supports ongoing pastoral changes by giving impulses for innovative church development. Analyzing the interfaces among these areas reveals concrete problems and shows viable solutions.

Starting with the administrative support pastors and priests expect, this paper will further analyze the problems general vicarages face regarding their administration. This topic ranges from the organization of professional and voluntary workers to the juridical support of parishes. Then, the special financial situation of the Catholic Church in Germany is considered. Regarding this, control and compliance are particular hot spots of recent challenges. The spiritualization of these areas is crucial for ineffective structures and processes. Third, the role of the general vicarage as an initiator of pastoral processes and an engine of innovation is more closely illuminated. Keywords here are digitalization and innovation through flexible structures that allow change to happen. Progression is more important than conservation. Finally, this paper will show how administration can support these ongoing processes, for example, by implementing a quality management system and other standards in the process of administrative work. All proposed actions should always answer to the vanishing point of pastoral work and support the proclamation of the gospel.

Pastors Need the Best Administrative Support

Many priests and pastors are overwhelmed by administrative responsibilities and therefore cannot focus on their pastoral mission. They find themselves more and more in the role of manager instead of being part of the pastoral team for the people. Tasks like human resource management, construction management, or accounting are not part of their theological education. This can be remedied by hiring a nonpastoral employee whose only responsibility is organizing the parish's administration, relieving the strain on the pastoral personnel, and leaving more resources to focus on the mission of the church. Since decentralization will be part of the future of the German Catholic Church, good coordination and organization is crucial if the church is to be present for believers. Realizing the importance of this relief, the Archdiocese of Cologne hired 180 administration managers, one for every priest in a leading position. Through this division of labor, the diocese hopes to establish more efficient pastoral teams that can focus on the church's mission.

In addition to the administrative challenges faced by priests, the numbers and the commitment of volunteers are dropping continuously. Many volunteers would rather perform short-term, low responsibility tasks than long-term administrative commitments. Reasons include a decrease in believers' disposable time due to work and other responsibilities as well as inefficient processes without digital support. By reorganizing and standardizing formal processes integrating the people into the system, the church could make these tasks more attractive for volunteers. For example, there could be accounting software with a smartphone app, integrating the work into the volunteers' preexisting digital environment. The trend of volunteers tending toward less responsible tasks is caused by the increasing complexity of the tasks and the responsibility becoming too much for an untrained volunteer. It feels too risky to take over one of these jobs in a parish. On the other hand, there are big risks for the church, if an untrained volunteer does one of these tasks, because the church has liability for actions others perform on its behalf. If risk is separated from workers, there is the moral hazard if they do not have to face the consequences of their actions. A solution could be to establish a structure like the Diocese of Essen established by centralizing responsibility for parish daycare centers. The aim of this kind of restructuring must always be better administration and a control system with everyone aware of their area of responsibility.

Not only volunteers, but also many employees working for the church lack solid knowledge regarding specific topics like taxes, employment law, process management, or office organization. These lacks lead insecurity within the administration, especially when there are complex changes in the law. A current challenge is the change of §2b in the value-added tax law. From 2021 on, parishes—because they are separate subunits—must pay value-added tax for services. Many parishes feel left alone by the dioceses, not knowing how to cope with this change. They ask for individual support from the general vicarage with customer-orientated and well-organized communication. The vicarages could and should respond with a specialized task force for this change, supporting their parishes with solid information.

These administrative challenges and examples of solutions affect all areas of the German Catholic Church's work. Everyone, from the volunteers to the vicar general, must prepare for fundamental changes regarding responsibility and their work in general. Distribution of tasks must be reconsidered and supported by modern and digital processes.

The Church Cannot Work without Money

Connected to questions regarding administration and responsibility is the question of church finances and property. The general vicarage is also mainly responsible for this crucial area. As shown in the introduction, the German Catholic Church is financially dependent on its believers as its main source of income. Due to the current good economic conditions, the church can still be compensated for losses due to the exodus of believers. But considering the unpredictability of the economy, the church will face financial problems in the future. Without efficient asset management, the core mission of the church, evangelization and presence for the people, is in danger. Thus, the highest priority should be preventing any kind of fraud and loss of control. Next, the aim should be efficient and sustainable asset management, oriented on ethical standards, securing the authenticity of the church.

General vicarages already often fail to prevent fraud, leading to big budget deficits. Church culture is one of blind trust without control mechanisms, even when decisions about huge amounts of money with substantial impact must be made. This system recently backfired in the Diocese of Eichstätt when the financial director misappropriated 60 million Euros through risky real estate investments in the United States. The lack of transparency allowed this director to freely invest the church's money without having to justify his decisions to anyone. The bishop has reacted to this scandal with multiple interventions for more transparency. First, the finance council of the diocese has been completely newly staffed. Instead of clerics without adequate knowledge in finance, external experts constitute the new council, reducing the risk of mismanagement. In a second step, the bishop separated the cathedral chapter from the ordinary conference to differentiate the controlling from the administrative board. Additionally, the diocesan administration will no longer be organized by a cleric but by a qualified leader who is associated to the vicar general. The aim is to establish governance structures in which everyone's responsibility is clear, and diffusion of responsibility is avoided. Lastly, the accounting standard should fulfill all criteria of the German Commercial Code. Regarding finances, the church is no different from other companies and thus should not be treated differently. Through these legal requirements and restructuring measures, a bishop can systematically fight against the kind of fraud that happened in Eichstätt.

The "trust-before-control" culture in many dioceses is even more problematic when the bishop himself is not interested in transparency. In Limburg, the ex-bishop was able to build an expensive residence costing 31 million Euros, bypassing all official boards. The members of the supervisory board were chosen by the bishop and were therefore very loyal and tolerant. Additionally, many of these members were not qualified to supervise. To avoid such structural weaknesses within a diocese, it is necessary to have well-qualified members on the boards. People on these supervisory boards should be independent of the bishop and be aware of their great responsibility for church finances. Therefore, the expectations should be high and include a basic understanding of finance and supervisory tasks.

Not only can boards make mistakes, but so can the multiple accounting authorities within a diocese. In the Archdiocese of Freiburg, the German pension insurance found irregularities regarding the contributions of the archdiocese. In many cases the accounting authorities made mistakes in contributions for the church's low-income service personnel, leading to tax evasion. As a precaution, the Archdiocese of Freiburg set aside 160 million Euros to cover unpaid social contributions and fines. This example shows that the Catholic Church sometimes acts as if it is above the law. This is a very risky attitude, and not just regarding finances. To avoid fines, tax evasion must be prevented by strict adherence to tax law. The church should think of itself like a regular company with obligations to fulfill like everyone else.

These three examples illustrate the lack of oversight in the Catholic Church, allowing fraud and mistakes to happen. Even without these manipulations, it is hard enough for many dioceses to cover costs and fulfill obligations. Efficient and farsighted asset management is not standard everywhere, leading to huge debts and less money for pastoral services even without fraud. A good example of this is the situation in the Archdiocese of Hamburg. After an external review by a consulting company, the vicar general announced the closure of eight of the twenty-one Catholic schools of the archdiocese, due to a deficit of 79 million Euros with the debt projected to increase to 353 million Euros in 2021, if no austerity was introduced. Past mismanagement inevitably led to a high backlog of investment in the schools and uncovered pension obligations for the staff. Closing these eight schools was the only way to save the others and leave resources for the church's mission. To focus on the church's mission, it is necessary for Hamburg—and many other dioceses—to practice economies. A good start is the presence of a small and efficient administration in the general vicarage.

After the scandal in the Diocese of Limburg, a transparency initiative was started by the church in Germany, disclosing diocesan finances. With the help of external experts, this transparency initiative revealed huge financial deficits and problems all over the German Catholic Church. In the future, these problems will worsen since the church tax revenue will decrease due to believers leaving the church or dying. The general vicarages are challenged to respond to this change by having controls to guard against fraud and arbitrariness on the one hand, and efficient and farsighted asset management for long-term survival on the other. From the financial point of view, the general vicarage must see itself as a normal company, which must at least cover its costs to fulfill its core mission. Employees working with the church's money should have a fundamental knowledge of finances. The bishop should understand himself not only as a shepherd, but also as a controller.

Concepts for Pastoral Progression Are Needed

The general vicarage not only functions as an administrative unit, but also has significant impact on the content of pastoral work. Administrative form and pastoral content are intertwined. The centralized diocesan vicarage is in a position to gather innovative ideas and spread them all over the diocese. Thus, it should develop concrete concepts for pastoral work and support new ways of evangelization. To cope with the rapidly changing world, many dioceses have started pastoral processes to adapt to the new situation. These are often initiated and coordinated by a small number of clerics, leading to a top-down mentality. This is problematic because believers are used to a democratic political system in which they have the right to discuss and vote for or against decisions. To avoid irritating and angering believers, it is crucial to develop a good concept with a clear timetable. Responsibilities need to be distributed and moderators designated before the process starts. Every process should ensure that those who will implement it get involved and prepared for their new tasks after the process is finalized. Otherwise, even the best concept, if created by only a few leaders, is worthless. Mediators between the general vicarage and the concrete pastoral contexts might support developments within a diocese. The role of the church's leaders and their administration should be that of enabling exchange and creating space for innovations, rather than actively prescribing the content of the process beforehand. Not realizing the importance of this base-focused approach to new processes, the Diocese of Würzburg faced enormous resistance when representatives of the general vicarage presented the first results of the process "Pastoral of the Future" to pastoral workers. The 130 members of the congress complained that there was insufficient communication during the process. In addition, a lay pastoral worker complained that the process responsibilities change too often. They felt left alone with their fears, while accompanying the restructuring measures the diocese faced, according to the bishop.

When one sees the vast numbers of people leaving the church, another deficit of many pastoral concepts is illuminated: they are not innovative enough. One reason is that most people active in the process grew up and lived in the recent pastoral system—and love it. They focus on keeping the status quo instead of the radically new. Of course, a pastoral process is always very emotional, especially since people must let go of cherished things. Thus, good concepts create room for the fears and doubts of believers and should try to translate these into creative energy. Apart from the believers' attitude, another reason for lack of progress is the church leaders themselves. Instead of developing a positive vision of their church, they establish a culture in which people fear making mistakes. Because of legalism, many innovative ideas are blocked before being tested. Therefore, many people would rather keep doing their jobs as they've always done rather than risk adverse consequences. This culture must change for any kind of innovation to happen. Innovation requires that people are enabled and pushed to try something new without fear of punishment if it does not work out. The need for this cultural change in management has become even more urgent since Pope Francis has been demanding it as well. The Diocese of Essen is setting a positive example here. Even though the diocese faces financial challenges, its leaders realized the importance of innovation and created a fund providing six million Euros for innovative ideas. The funding is limited to a maximum of three years per project. For instance, one funded idea came from a priest working in hospital ministry. He developed a system to identify patients needing the most pastoral attention based on data supplied by the hospital. With the help of the innovation fund, six employees are payed to analyze the concrete demands of the patients. Afterward, they guide the many volunteers who visit patients. In this case the fund helped to increase the pastoral team from one priest to twenty people, with the priest as coordinator. To spread this idea, a congress with participants from other dioceses was held, but too frequently there are no structures to share innovative ideas like this. The general vicarage needs to find ways to share innovative ideas with other parishes and dioceses.

Departments within a diocese often have no connection or efficient means of communication. This problem exists both regarding communication within the church and communication to believers. Here, the church should take advantage of ongoing digital innovation. The general vicarage should establish a legally sound infrastructure for digital pastoral work. The pastoral teams not only need technology, but also the competence to use it efficiently. Instead of demonizing modern technologies, the church should take advantage of them. Realizing the importance of the new ways of communication, the Bishop of Hamburg created his own WhatsApp chat, allowing anyone to easily get in touch with him. He regularly sends updates of his work, including selfies and inspirational texts. The 1,300 registered users can also ask any questions they want, which are then answered by the bishop or his representative. Using WhatsApp in this way is an innovative way to cope with current circumstances, including in youth ministry.

To have successful pastoral concepts, good working communication is key. Church leaders, who historically have relied on their authority to establish new ideas, will only be successful shepherds if they dialogue with believers. In a complex world, new concepts for pastoral work cannot be created by closed boards of ten people. The more people who are integrated into the process by efficient communication using digital resources, the more successful a pastoral process can be. For this to happen, a culture of fear needs to give way to a culture of trust, where innovative ideas can grow from the bottom up instead of being implemented top-down.

Pastoral Development Must Be Supported

In order to support continuously changing ministry with pastoral processes, the general vicarage must be highly adaptable as well. General vicarages tend to be very sluggish, working the same way as many years before. Changes only happen very slowly, speeding up only when financial or public pressure is high enough. Many in the church feel that everything works fine and live in self-deception. They do not see the importance of change. But as shown before, many dioceses are struggling with their finances. By openly admitting these problems, a diocese can emphasize the need for action to their believers. The Diocese of Essen attaches importance to financial transparency. Therefore, it publishes a balance sheet like a normal company. The profit and loss statement for 2017 shows an annual loss of 8.9 million Euros. Like Essen, more and more dioceses are publishing their balance sheets, a great step toward more transparency. Most of the balance sheets meet the standards of the German Commercial Code. Only nine meet the standards completely. Thus, the next step should be not only to have balance sheets for every diocese, but also to conform them to the German Commercial Code. By doing this, the budgets of all twenty-seven dioceses could be compared. The wealthier dioceses, in solidarity, should then support poorer dioceses like Essen or those in eastern Germany. To attain this, transparency on the highest possible level is necessary. However, at the same time, this support should not veil the importance of process.

In addition to ignorance of financial pressure and need for change, often enough innovative ideas are blocked by high formal hurdles set up by people who do not see the need to act and doubt their efficiency. In challenging times like these, the general vicarage should show its openness to innovation by supporting new attempts within the diocese. Recently, the Diocese of Freiburg has been supportive of the deanery in Mannheim, where the dean manages his own processes. The aim of this is to centralize multiple pastoral tasks in one area of the city. In other parishes, these services will no longer be provided. Thus, the deanery can still offer a vast range of pastoral work, by having ministries for baptism and youth in centralized places instead of having small ministries in every single parish. This specialization requires openness and flexibility, not only from the people, but also from the administration, which must offer structural support, for instance changing employee schedules and better coordinating different parishes. Even though this process is exhausting, without innovation, the deanery of Mannheim would fall into lethargy.

No one knows where this process will lead; it requires an administration that can adapt. At worst, a meaningful process might be undermined by inefficient administration. Thus, transformation of the administration should be standard, not exceptional. Dioceses could be inspired by agile companies in organizing the next confirmation, the next pastoral process, or even something as big as the German Catholic Day by using the "scrum method." For example, German Catholic Day is an event held by the German Catholic Church every two years. Over thirty thousand participants gather to pray, discuss, and meet for five days, and the cities that host this event change each time. In the scrum method, big projects like this are divided into smaller pieces, which are then worked on in small sprints. Everyone can see the status of the work all the time, and after a sprint has finished, the next piece is done in another sprint. It is very important to have constant communication, and the process needs to be planned backward from the goal. These goals should be specific, measurable, achievable, reasonable, and time-bound (SMART). Before making any strategic decisions, the general vicarage should think about the goal to be reached. Instead of controlling the input, the focus should be on output of projects. Thus, the general vicarage must give decision aids for pastoral decisions in subunits of the diocese. To control output and get constant feedback on the work, the general vicarage should establish regular evaluations and quality management. Quality management has not really been implemented in the church yet, but it can be a good tool toward more efficient use of resources.

So far, the Catholic Church in Germany is only at the beginning of focusing on output control. Many resources are often put into pastoral work without checking and adapting to the outcome. Through the total quality management in hospitals, clinic ministry was the first area of pastoral work to get quality management. In the meantime, the Diocese of Münster has implemented a quality management system for their Catholic schools to improve the quality of their ministry. Having a well-working quality management system, not only in ministry but also in the general vicarage, could ensure a constant drive for change and development. Pastoral decisions that should be supported by the general vicarage must not be made without knowing the available resources.

A New Relationship Must Be Formed

These new perspectives on administrative work as basis for ministry can be summarized and connected with six theses for church administration. First, digitalization would reduce the resources for administrative work and allow more people to participate. Discovering the potential of digitalization opens completely new ways for the church to reconnect with people who have turned their backs on the church. These new channels need to be combined with a new openness for innovation to adapt to the new situations. Digitalization itself is not the complete solution for every problem of the church, but it can help to reform pastoral work enormously by shifting more human resources toward ministry on the one hand and connecting the church with the world on the other. By using new forms of communication, for example social media such as WhatsApp or Twitter, the church can stay in contact with the next generation and be inspired by their view of the world. For reform to take place, structures then must be responsive to innovative ideas and the administration must be very flexible to let those ideas infiltrate, grow, be tested, and implemented if they work. This can be supported by digitized process management and a culture of courage.

Second, the German Church should reflect on what tasks needs to be done by individual parishes and what services could be handed over to the diocese in order to professionalize these services. Respecting the principle of subsidiarity, priorities need to be established in the cooperation between parishes and general vicarages. By specializing and professionalizing services, the created synergies help to emphasize pastoral work and channel resources more efficiently. A great way of implementing this new form of cooperation is the establishment of administrative managers as in the Diocese of Cologne. Priests can easily be relieved of administrative tasks by professionals. In addition, for voluntary work the reorganization of services is crucial since more and more volunteers can take over responsibility for highly complex tasks.

Third, connected to the revised distribution of tasks is the updating of the tasks themselves. Many services are traditionally offered by the church but no longer needed. A reevaluation of the services through standardized quality management systems can help identify what's outdated. For this to happen, the perspective of pastoral work must shift from an input focus to prioritizing the outcome. Regarding this, it might be helpful to think of the believers as customers, even though this term needs to be used carefully since the church is not only a service provider. Once different "customer groups" (adults, singles, married, elderly, refugees) are identified, adequate services need to be found and supplied by either the parishes or the general vicarages. Every service needs to be examined to see whether it is important and which institution can offer it best.

Fourth, a completely new relationship between general vicarage and the parishes must be developed. The general vicarage must see itself as administrative partner of the parishes rather than an authority. A new way of thinking is needed in a new world of living. Diocesan administration, including the vicar general and the bishop, should no longer see themselves as the heads who lead everything. Instead, a more cooperative way of interaction and communication is required on every level. By understanding the general vicarage as an eye-level partner for deaneries and parishes, more participation should be enabled. The pastoral process of Mannheim is a good example to show that slowly, but surely, church leaders are trying to put these structures into reality. But this learning process is still in the beginning and needs to be enforced looking into the future. Some movements within the church even propose a synodal structure, which would totally change the way the church works.

Fifth, the administration needs a boost of professionalization and an orientation to industry standards. This applies especially to ecclesiastical property and finance management. For tasks like finance, management, or accounting, religion should not be a selection criterion for staffing. There is no Catholic accounting that would allow exceptions. For maximum transparency, church finance needs to be treated like that in a normal company. This includes a balance sheet conforming to the German Commercial Code. What applies to Catholic hospitals, where religion is no criteria for appropriate treatment, also applies to Catholic administration. Thus, for people to work for the church, fundamental knowledge regarding the area of work is much more important than religiousness. Controlling and standardized processes are efficient instruments to secure the economic survival of the diocese in the long run, enabling more freedom for pastoral work. Additionally, the trust-before-control culture needs to be repressed by a culture of controlling, clear processes, and responsibility.

The bishop should not only see himself as a shepherd but also as a controller and, if necessary, enforce the discipline himself. After the financial scandal in Eichstätt, the bishop realized that some people actively tried to falsify information and that consensus is not always the best way to lead a diocese. To avoid fraud, regulatory structures are indispensable.

Finally, the structure of the administration of the future must be flexible and adaptive to keep up with the changes in the world. Mandatory standards must be established and—more importantly—lived by the people creating them. The flexibility of the administration starts in the minds of the people working within it. Thus, a new culture of flexibility and trust regarding innovation and change is highly recommended for an administration of the future to be adaptable. The general vicarage should understand itself as proactive creator of change into the future instead of a passive victim of changing circumstances. Digitalization will shape the world to yet unknown dimensions. An administration unable to keep in touch with this reality will more and more lose connection to its associated pastoral teams in the parishes and lose itself in self-referential work.

5

Silent Contracts

Implicature, Parish Leadership Style, and Parishioner Engagement

Marti R. Jewell

We need effective leadership now more than ever as we explore how to be church in a postpandemic world. As pastoral leaders, we are called to bring God's people into the mission of Christ. There is no debate about this, but dissonance abounds around who Catholic pastoral leaders are and what they need to do to achieve this mission. While we talk a lot about leadership, we spend little time preparing for it and less developing the skills needed by pastors, permanent deacons, and lay ecclesial ministers. In these days of rapid change in parish life, research has shown us that one's understanding and practice of leadership can make a difference in how effective our leadership can be.

So what *is* a leader? The one in charge? The one who ensures the parish is functioning properly? Maybe the one who animates the faith community? In a study by the *Emerging Models of Pastoral Leadership Project*[1] three pastoral leadership styles surfaced, each with a distinct set of expectations, ecclesiology, and pastoral relationships. This *Project* called together over five hundred lay and ordained pastoral leaders from across the United States, as well as parishioners on parish pastoral councils, asking them to share their understanding of pastoral leadership and how it functions. In analyzing their responses, differing understandings of leadership surfaced. Furthermore, it also became evident that one's understanding of leadership is a predictor of their particular struggles as well as their impact on the parish, staff, and parishioners.

Where leaders use a hierarchical style of leadership, parishioners respond by expecting to be cared for. Where the leaders have created a culture of shared leadership serving the parish, parishioners respond by expecting services. Where pastoral leaders animate the leadership of parishioners, they see the development of missionary disciples. Problems arise, then, when leadership styles clash with parishioner expectations. This research suggests that by examining these leadership styles and the implicit agreements between leaders and parishioners, we can better understand what is happening and how to respond. So what are these "implicit agreements"?

Silent Contracts

How-to books on leadership tend to be written by, to, and for the leader, but this is only half of the equation. Leaders have followers and how they interact with each other is rarely a subject of research. Different styles of leadership elicit predictable responses from followers even as the expectations and behavior of followers impact the ability of leaders to lead. What has been missing from much of today's leadership research and advice is the "view from the pew." Studies from the vantage point of followers are only newly being explored by business and church studies and are sorely needed. In a 2010 global survey by IBM, CEOs describe how the old, traditional business models and ways of leading no longer work. Customers now drive the conversation, and leaders must focus on the customers. This realization "will require entirely new leadership styles, new approaches to better understanding our customers, and new and flexible structures for their businesses."[2]

It is no different for church leadership. In church circles, leadership has rarely been questioned, at least until now, and its impact on parish staff and parishioners even less so. We know that—much like the familiar iceberg metaphor—there is a lot going on beneath the surface in parish life, unseen, unspoken but very real, impacting the health of the community. How we respond to this as pastoral leaders, in any given situation, is learned uncritically at an early age, learning meant to maintain social relationships.

This concept was explored by Dr. H. P. Grice, who defined the concept of implicature, a way of explaining the way people respond to what is not spoken.[3] According to this theory, people just seem to know how to behave, how to engage in interactions with other people, or behave in different settings without anyone having to tell us how to do so. When someone "misbehaves" or doesn't comply with expectations, everyone is upset. This phenomenon has also been studied by transactional analysts who posit that human beings have unspoken, even unconscious responses to situations.[4] The idea followed a concept popularized in the 1960s by psychologist Eric Berne, who wrote, "If two people encounter each other...sooner or later one of them will speak or give some other indication of acknowledging the presence of the others. This is called *transactional stimulus*....Another person will then say or do something which is in some way related to the stimulus, and this is called the *transactional response*."[5] What's more, we are learning these responses are not a one-way street. Leaders are equally influenced by followers who place unspoken expectations on their behavior.[6]

These are the silent contracts to which I refer, the unspoken but assumed interactions between pastoral leaders and staff of parishioners. They exist at every level and this idea of implicature is well documented in the *Emerging Models* data. Think of parishioners, for example, who put the pastor on a pedestal, and get upset if he doesn't live up to their expectations. Or the young priest who quickly realizes that the moment he voices his opinion, that will be the end of the discussion because of parishioners who assume that Father knows best, even though no one ever discussed this belief and response. This is implicature in action.

Here, I offer findings from the *Emerging Models of Pastoral Leadership Project*, which documented leadership experiences and beliefs of both pastoral leaders and parishioners. I will introduce the styles in parish ministry we encountered, their impact on parishioners in their own words, and the consequences for pastoral leaders and parish vitality, hopefully shedding some light on these silent contracts in order for leaders to adapt styles that will lead to better parishioner engagement.

As we begin, keep several points in mind. First, please note that while our first impulse may be to assume this paper is about the pastor—and it does include him—these styles are employed by any person in a leadership position...youth minister, catechetical leader, principal, pastoral council chair, or bishop. Second, the leadership styles presented here are developmental, each engaging and impacting ever-larger numbers of people. At the same time, they are concentric in that the tasks of each style are included in the next. Third, all these styles are situational and, in practice, leaders can move back and forth between them. Finally, the observations of parishioners, some of which are shared here, are both noteworthy in how well parishioners understand the leadership dynamics in their parish, and revelatory in showing these contracts at work.

Style 1: Leadership Focused in the Leader

The first and most familiar leadership style focuses on the leader, the one in the C-suite, the one ranked higher on the hierarchical ladder. This leader is concerned with their own leadership abilities and responsibilities. Sometimes called autocratic or parental leaders, the weight of leadership lies heavily on their shoulders. These traditional CEO types depend on their personal training and experience, sometimes consulting to gather input, while feeling personally responsible for all that happens. They see themselves as holding and exercising power. Sometimes this style is based on a misreading of canon law, conflating governance with leadership, believing only the pastor can be the leader. As recognized by one parishioner, "Our model [of leadership] is still very much in control by the pastor. The pastoral council is partly hand-picked by him. Others are invited, but he is in total control."[7] This thinking can be mirrored at other levels, so that the pastoral associate or youth minister will adopt a hierarchical leadership style, making all decisions within their purview, sometimes consulting, but rarely letting go.

Hierarchical Leadership

The unspoken contract for the age-old style of hierarchical leadership maintains what has been called a parent-child relationship between the leader and those he or she is leading, traditionally expecting followers (and they are seen as followers) to respond with loyalty and faithful obedience. In turn, parishioners come expecting to be cared for. You might say, if you treat people like children they will act like children. Another metaphor for hierarchical leadership was captured by Pope Francis when he spoke about church as a field hospital ready to do triage after a battle.[8] The leaders are the surgeons and medics to whom people come for healing and care. The leaders are the ones with the knowledge; the hurting are the recipients of their ministrations.

For parishioners, this unspoken agreement seems to say they only need to come for Mass but otherwise don't need to be involved in the parish. They do, however, expect the pastor to show up whenever they need him, especially at hospitals, sick beds, and funerals. After all they have been obedient children, giving whatever was asked. Now they expect to collect on that "silent contract." When told that Father can't come because it is his day off, or the DRE won't schedule another baptism prep class at a more convenient time, parishioners feel the contract has been broken and feel alienated. Only, we never say it in these words because these are, after all, *silent* contracts. It is these silent contracts that have kept parishioners quietly participating, albeit unknowingly, in a clerical culture that believes that the pastor, or pastoral leaders, cannot be challenged.

Pastoral leaders operating with this style have definite, often implicit, expectations of the staff, council, or core team they work with. We can see an example of this in the pastor who meets regularly with staff or council members, asking their opinions about issues but then doing as he pleases, sometimes only asking because it is expected. Council members and staff offer advice, hoping it will be taken. In the words of one respondent to the *Emerging Models* research, "Our finance council relates well with the pastor. He takes our recommendations into consideration. He has the last say, but he weighs our recommendations heavily."[9]

There is a shadow side to this style of leadership. Working with a hierarchical leader, sometimes a micromanager, leads to staff members becoming frustrated, growing increasingly disrespected, eventually disconnecting and isolating. It shows up in restless parish council members who come thinking their experience and expertise are valued only to discover they are not. It shows up as parishioners who are counted among the "Dones" and the "Almost Dones," those adults who are simply not showing up anymore. What people are "done" with is being treated as children, the silent contract of this model. And this works both ways. Parishioners who seem to have stopped honoring the silent contract leave pastoral leaders hurt and confused. One young seminarian asked, in all honesty, why people didn't do as he told them. Studies have shown this style of leadership is the least effective, with dominance seen as being different from leadership, often undermining relationships and outcomes.[10]

If our objective is to share in the mission of Christ, not just ourselves but forming the whole community to do so, then it is up to us to find the most effective and efficient way to do so. Hierarchical models of leadership, these lone ranger leaders, are the least effective, and in fact have become problematic in parishes as well as industry. One way to move forward is to develop and work with core teams so that together they can have a greater impact.

Style 2: Leadership Focused in a Core Team

A pastoral leader working with a designated core team of staff or volunteers in serving the community represents the second style of leadership expressed by the *Emerging Models* participants. Here core teams share in the responsibility of leadership, authorized to provide programming and ministry, and oversee the sacramental life of the community. There are certainly a variety of staffing models in U.S. parishes, from large staff made up of permanent deacons, lay ecclesial ministers, lay professionals, and school personnel, to small rural parishes with no resident pastor or staff, dependent on parishioners. There is even the rare parochial vicar. Developing trust and intentional team formation provide the key to the success of effective leadership. Co-responsibility is important here. One *Emerging Models* respondent stated that the "pastor's leadership is one of openness, collaboration, delegation, and empowerment of others. It's a 'we' approach, not an 'I' approach."[11] Described well by Chris Fussell in *One Mission*, members of effective teams "trust one another... bound by a common sense of purpose...and a sense of shared consciousness," authorized to make decisions related to their role and expertise.[12] While we have long used the classical, Thomistic/ Aristotelian ranked style of leadership,[13] team leadership is more theological. We are a trinitarian church, relational in nature. It is through the self-giving of the Son that the Father reached earth, and their love continues in the Spirit promised by Jesus. It is in the idea of relational self-giving that we find this model of leadership.

Servant Leadership

In the research, leaders working with core teams described themselves as servant leaders, truly caring for their parishioners. According to one pastor, "They see themselves as enablers and servants to the parish."[14] The concept of servant leadership has been developed by ethics professor Robert Greenleaf, who believes that the "servant-leader *is* servant *first*. It begins with the natural feeling that one wants to serve, to serve first. Then conscious choice brings one to aspire to lead. That person is sharply different from one that is *leader* first."[15] Here the leadership dynamic has changed to one of shared power predicated on the belief that more can get done if there is a larger group of leaders. When power is shared or distributed, recipients have both the responsibility and the authority to do what is expected of them. This is seen in parishes that have an active core team working with, and supported by, the pastor. It can as easily be seen in the youth minister working with a core team of parents, or a catechetical leader working with a faith formation committee.

Team members work as peers, ministering out of shared vision and trust, essential to this form of leadership. According to one pastoral leader, "A key behavior to successful parish operations, parish leaders need to ensure teaming and collaboration among parish staff, lay leaders, and parish organizations (e.g., school staff). This is effected by cross organization representation, group leadership meetings, and an atmosphere of sharing."[16] In order to achieve this kind of teamwork, parish teams find they must work hard to create and maintain their ability to work together while striving to involve parishioners, seen as volunteers or helpers, in their ministry. This serves the parish well. Research has shown that where there is greater follower (team) involvement in decision-making, organizations can be more effective.[17]

There are two separate challenges in this style of leadership: one between leader and team, the other between team and parishioners, both often unspoken and unexamined. The first has to do with an understanding of how power is shared between leader and team, and calls for letting go of the implicit belief that power is a zero-sum game, which is understood to mean the more you give away the less you have. One must let go of the idea of having power over a team and move toward the idea of providing the team with the power to do that which they are charged to do.[18] Make no mistake. Sharing power can be difficult. It can seem as if the leader is giving away their role and authority. In practice, the opposite seems to be true. Those who delegate power are seen as powerful due to increased respect and trust, critical components of shared power. This leads to the use of subsidiarity and the authorization of those closest to their ministry to make decisions. The more work done by the team and leader to build trust and a shared vision, the more this can happen. The more it happens, the greater the effect on parish work.

This sets up the second challenge for parish staff and focuses on how they, in turn, use their authority. According to Greenleaf, as lived out in parishes, servant leaders take care to "make sure that other people's highest priority needs are being served."[19] Where providing for the needs of, and services to, parishioners is the focus, leadership comes to be understood as having the power (meaning authority and responsibility) to produce results. In practice, pastoral staff meeting these demands begin to speak of "our" programs, seeing it as their responsibility to provide for the parish, and consequently see parishioners as volunteers helping them out as they serve the needs of the parish. As one parishioner aptly noted, the parish staff "are often the 'doers' rather than the stewards of talents and wisdom in the parish."[20] This flows from an implicit institutional model of church in which leadership is about maintaining and providing for the ongoing life of the parish. Consequently, an unspoken contract is set up in which parishioners expect the parish to provide for their needs, feeling quite validated in asking, "What is the parish doing for me?" To meet these requests, parishes have come to have sixty, seventy, or eighty different ministries going on at any given time. This is a "Walmart" image of parish where parishioners come expecting a menu of options, a variety of times and accessibility, and if they do not find what they want, they feel quite justified in being critical or parish shopping.

For their part, teams develop an expectation that parishioners should help provide the services needed in their own parish. Where parishioners aren't appropriately involved and grateful, leaders can be alternately disgusted with their response or anxious because they somehow failed to find the magic formula for serving the parish. What then happens is well described by one parishioner: "There are many ministries and activities taking place in the parish, but often the same faces are in the majority at these events. That's not necessarily bad, but without some sort of cohesive vision, they remain a group of faith-filled people moving in and out of parish functions without experiencing transformation."[21] This respondent has seen the difference between services and formation. Another, also recognizing this, stated, "Our parish is more an aggregation of activities rather than a community pursuing the mission of church."[22]

The implicit agreement here becomes clear. Parishioners expect services and ought to volunteer; pastoral leaders are expected to provide them. Surveys of parish teams bear this out. Research has shown that parish leaders see themselves as more successful at encouraging involvement and promoting parish services than in listening and sharing decision-making roles.[23] This is characteristic of this style of leadership. One young youth minister discovered, to her dismay, that she was so involved in putting on programs, she had lost track of her need to be in ministry to the teens in her youth group.[24] The way to move forward would be to see these services, not as ends in and of themselves, but as the means to the end of forming community, the goal of the third leadership style encountered by the *Emerging Models Project*.

Style 3: Leadership Focus on the Community

Creating a vital parish as an open and welcoming community, where people have a strong sense of belonging, is the top priority for two-thirds of U.S. Catholics responding to surveys conducted by the Center for Applied Research in the Apostolate (CARA).[25] This is true regardless of race or ethnicity. At heart, this reflects church as *communio*, understood here to be an ecclesiology of communion and mission, in which all are called to live out their baptismal call to discipleship. One parishioner described their understanding in very practical terms: "Big or small, the parish of the future will realize that the people truly are the church, and what happens in their church is on their shoulders, good or bad, it is theirs."[26] The ability to animate such a community marks the third style of leadership that surfaced in the *Emerging Models* research: leadership whose focus and attention is the community itself. An example of this is one parish located in a transitional neighborhood. This community, after parish-wide discernment, decided to provide only essential programming while parishioners, then, intentionally engage in service to the neighborhood, helping the poor and elderly as well as young families. This approach has been met with high success in terms of growing parishioner engagement.[27]

What is unique to this leadership style is the primary focus on parishioners, animating their gifts and forming them for missionary discipleship both within the parish and beyond. The work of the parish is now the means to an end—forming disciples—rather than an end in itself. It reflects the growing sense of church that marks many of today's Catholics. As noted by one *Emerging Models* respondent, the "pray, pay, and obey concept is dying....Community members are not afraid to take responsibility in a variety of ways, e.g., liturgical life, spiritual formation, and service projects."[28] The significance of this style of leadership is that it draws on the wisdom of the community, leaders and parishioners together finding the best way to live out the mission of the church, in their place and time.

Animating Leadership

Pastoral leaders who are focused on impacting the community act as catalysts in calling forth and engaging the gifts and leadership of parishioners, one of the benchmarks for a vital and healthy parish according to the *Emerging Models* studies. "This emerging role of pastoral staff often includes calling forth and mentoring the gifts of others beyond day-to-day direct ministry they provide to members of the parish."[29]

This is a transformational leadership model that, "unlike traditional leadership approaches (where the emphasis may be on a top-down power and control relationship), the transformational leader has the ability to inspire and motivate group members."[30] According to theorist Bernard M. Bass, transformational leaders "stimulate and inspire followers to achieve extraordinary outcomes, and in the process develop their own leadership capacity....They respond to individual followers' needs by empowering them and aligning [them with] the goals of the organization."[31] This best matches the call of today's church to create dynamic disciples.

When leaders focus on animating the community for mission, their leadership is understood, not as who one is (hierarchical) or what one does (institutional), but as how one impacts the community (*communio*). As described by one pastoral associate, "We support one another and call forth gifts in the community. We challenge the lay leadership [parishioners] with mission, accountability and creating community."[32] One pastor called it "a facilitating leadership."[33]

Also called adaptive leadership, coming from a concept developed by Harvard School of Business professors Ronald Heifetz and Marty Linsky,[34] this style recognizes the need to engage communities in the process of change, and is described as "the practice of mobilizing people to tackle tough challenges and thrive."[35] Heifetz and Linsky will tell you this is not an easy task. "Adaptive problems are challenges for which there are no easy answers. They are not amenable to authoritarian or standard operating procedures. They cannot be solved by someone who provides answers from on high."[36] Yet today's parish challenges call for leaders who hold a view of the totality, complexity, and interdependence of the community, a vision to which they are deeply committed, and are willing to adapt their leadership style to make these communities successful.

When pastor and staff work together to animate the community, in effect animating the baptismal call to mission, an entirely different set of demands is placed on both pastoral leaders and parishioners. In the words of one parishioner, "Healthy parishes will be characterized by a total ministering community of pastors, staff, and parishioners working together. What will change are the roles of each."[37] Another parishioner recognized this leadership style and its implications this way: "Mission-based; more fluid—less structure; appreciation of diversity; outward focus—community view; engage a world view."[38] Being intentional about calling forth the gifts of parishioners and developing missionary disciples calls for strategic action. According to one pastor, "The parish is growing in the sense of self as gifted and capable. We have approximately 70 people in leadership positions. Not everyone is called to leadership, though everyone is called to ministry. We continuously discern who in the community is being moved by the spirit into leadership."[39]

This empowerment is accomplished by activities such as developing and owning a parish mission statement; providing facilitation for a variety of ministries, councils, or commissions; surveys and town halls; all working together to articulate a vision for a particular parish. The new demands on the community call for a change of heart by both pastoral staff and parishioners. According to one parishioner, "More people in the parish community are coming to realize that the changes in the 'church' as a whole are affecting how a church community will function because of the difficulties in leadership and, therefore, are becoming more curious and maybe more willing to 'step up to the plate and go to bat' for the parish community."[40]

Significant questions arise in the use of this style of leadership. When animating the leadership of others, do pastoral leaders give up leadership? In fact, the answer is no they don't. But it does have its challenges. Pastoral leaders must let go of doing everything themselves and become the catalyst by calling forth the leadership of others. As one participant put it, "The staff serves as guides, mentors, support, liaisons, again empowering others to take the ball and run, knowing that others are there for encouragement and support. Often the staff are the ones who provide the personal invitation to parishioners to become leaders."[41] This is not an easy task. It may feel like a loss. Here the implicit contract makes new and unexpected demands, requiring a redefinition of one's identity as a leader.[42] This takes maturity, experience, and intention, but is rooted in the call to create missionary disciples.

Parishioners are equally challenged in this new contract. They are expected to take ownership for their parish, for their interactions with one another, and for taking their faith out into the world. This is no longer just "Father's job" but now belongs to all members of the faith community, pastor, staff, and parishioner alike. One pastor describes it this way: "Sharing their gifts within the community, but more importantly, sharing beyond. Stepping forth as council, commissions, finance committee, etc., to share the mission of Jesus in the parish; leaders in the greater community in the world inviting people to know Jesus and of the importance of working for him and worship."[43] Where this has not been the expected behavior, it will have to be taught, even though, as one parishioner put it, "lay people seem comfortable with the traditional model. There has not been enough education as to other models. There has been no demand for change."[44] Parishioners do recognize the need, as one parish pastoral councilor stated, for "overcoming resistance to change; overcoming parochialism; re-educating the whole community, including pastors; creating the challenges for the community to rise up to the challenge; being able to be Christ to each other in a community; keep Christ at the center of our focus."[45] This is the epitome of good leadership. We must move forward, forming communities of belonging and mission, *communio*; our mission to engage parishioners in the covenant to which we are called.

Conclusion

Animating missionary disciples focused on the mission of Christ, the end to which we are called, is about real human beings, engaged in the eschatological mission of the church to move toward community, conversion, and mission. The pastoral leaders encountered by the *Emerging Models Project* showed deep fidelity to their ministry and to the people of God, doing so in the face of growing and intense challenges. They hold a vision for a church that is more committed to collaboration and shared leadership, with an increased role of the laity in the life of the parish. As described by one parishioner, "Regardless of the number of priests, active parishioners want a voice. Our challenge is to provide direction and focus to the voice. Empowerment only exists in an environment that supports it: vision, boundaries, skills, and commitment. We can share leadership within a model governed by a priest—where each leader works together based upon their gifts. All leaders must also demonstrate accountability for their part, even while acknowledging the priest's overall accountability."[46]

While it can seem easier to do the work oneself, not dealing with the relational challenges of working with others or forming a community, in the end this is what we are called to do. Working together we are more than any one of us can be on our own. If we truly hope to form missionary disciples, we must accept Pope Francis's challenge to renew pastoral structures "as part of an effort to make them more mission-oriented, to make ordinary pastoral activity on every level more inclusive and open, to inspire in pastoral workers a constant desire to go forth and in his way elicit a positive response from all those whom Jesus summons to friendship with himself."[47] This is the hope to which we are all called.

Are we willing to accept the challenge, turning silent contracts into covenants with God's people? Change takes great courage and compassion. It takes admitting that the old forms are dying away, no longer sustainable. The Holy Spirit is calling us into an unanticipated future. The choice is ours. Can we find the courage and creativity to be the best leaders and parishioners we can be?

Notes

1. The "Emerging Models of Pastoral Leadership Project" was a joint research effort of the National Association for Lay Ministry, Conference for Pastoral Planning and Council Development, National Catholic Young Adult Ministry Association, National Association of Church Personnel Administrators, National Association of Diaconate Directors, and Nation Federation of Priests' Councils, funded by the Lilly Endowment, Inc., in their Sustaining Pastoral Excellence Program. Results of these studies can be accessed in the *Emerging Models of Pastoral Leadership Series* published by Loyola Press.

2. *Capitalizing on Complexity: Insights from the Global Chief Executive Office Study* (Somers, NY: IBM Global Business Services, 2010), 14–15.

3. Wayne Davis, "Implicature," *The Stanford Encyclopedia of Philosophy* (Fall 2014 Edition), ed. Edward N. Zalta, accessed June 4, 2018, https://plato.stanford.edu/archives/fall2014/entries/implicature/.

4. Ronald A. Heifetz, *Leadership without Easy Answers* (Cambridge, MA: Harvard University Press, 1998), 5.

5. Eric Berne, *Games People Play* (New York: Grove Press, 1964), 29. Italics in original.

6. Edwin Hollander and Lynn Offermann, "Power Leadership in Organizations: Relationships in Transition," *American Psychologist* 45, no. 2 (1990): 179–80.

7. David Ramey, "Emerging Models of Pastoral Leadership: Northeast Regional Symposium Report," June 23–25, 2005, 17, https://cdn.ymaws.com/www.nalm.org/resource/resmgr/documents/emergingmodels/regionalreports/northeast-symposium-final-re.pdf.

8. Robert Barron, "The Field Hospital Is Open: Reflections on Pope Francis' Interview," *Catholic News Agency*, October 2, 2013, accessed May 30, 2018, https://www.catholicnewsagency.com/column/the-field-hospital-is-open-reflections-on-pope-francis-interview-2692.

9. Emerging Models of Pastoral Leadership Project, *The Role and Reality of Parish Business Managers and Parish Finance Council Members FINAL Report* (Washington, DC: NALM, 2012), 49.

10. Hollander and Offermann, "Power Leadership," 179.

11. David Ramey, "Emerging Models of Pastoral Leadership: South Regional Symposium Report," October 3–5, 2006, 24, https://cdn.ymaws.com/www.nalm.org/resource/resmgr/documents/emergingmodels/regionalreports/south-symposium-final-report.pdf.

12. Chris Fussell and C. W. Goodyear, *One Mission: How Leaders Build a Team of Teams* (New York: Portfolio/Penguin, 2017), 1–2.

13. Ilia Delio, *The Emergent Christ* (Maryknoll, NY: Orbis Books, 2011), 114–15.

14. Ramey, "South," 26.

15. Robert K. Greenleaf, *Servant Leadership: A Journey into the Nature of Legitimate Power and Greatness* (New York: Paulist Press, 1977), 13. Italics in original.

16. David Ramey, "Emerging Models of Pastoral Leadership: Upper Midwest Regional Symposium Report," November 18–20, 2004, 68, https://cdn.ymaws.com/www.nalm.org/resource/resmgr/documents/emergingmodels/regionalreports/upper-midwest-symposium-summ.pdf.

17. Hollander and Offermann, "Power in Leadership," 183.

18. Greenleaf, *Servant Leadership*, 41.

19. Greenleaf, *Servant Leadership*, 13.

20. Ramey, "Upper Midwest," 29.

21. David Ramey, "Emerging Models of Pastoral Leadership: Mid-Atlantic Regional Symposium Report," November 2–4, 2005, 18, https://cdn.ymaws.com/www.nalm.org/resource/resmgr/documents/emergingmodels/regionalreports/mid-atlantic-symposium-final.pdf.

22. Ramey, "Northeast," 20.

23. Charles E. Zech et al., *Catholic Parishes of the 21st Century* (New York: Oxford University Press, 2017), 64.

24. Private conversation.

25. Zech, *Catholic Parishes*, 122.

26. Ramey, "South," 59.

27. Private conversation.

28. Ramey, "South," 28.

29. Jewell and Ramey, *Changing Face*, 119.

30. Joseph R. Ferrari, "Called and Formed: Personality Dimensions and Leadership Styles among Catholic Deacons and Men in Formation," *Pastoral Psychology* 66 (2017): 225–37, 226.

31. Bernard M. Bass and Ronald E. Riggio, *Transformational Leadership*, 2nd ed. (London: Lawrence Erlbaum Associates, 2005), 3.

32. Ramey, "Upper Midwest," 23.

33. Ramey, "Northeast," 21.

34. See Heifetz, *Leadership without Easy Answers*.

35. Ronald Heifetz and Marty Linsky, *The Practice of Adaptive Leadership: Tools and Tactics for Adapting Your Organization and the World* (Cambridge, MA: Harvard Business Review Press, 2009), 14.

36. Heifetz, *Leadership without Easy Answers*, 13.

37. Ramey, "Midwest," 43.

38. Ramey, "Midwest," 57.

39. Ramey, "Mid-Atlantic," 3.

40. Ramey, "Mid-Atlantic," 36.

41. Ramey, "South," 27.

42. Heifetz, *Leadership without Easy Answers*, 30.

43. Ramey, "Upper Midwest," 30.

44. Ramey, "Northeast," 34.

45. Ramey, "Northeast," 47.

46. Ramey, "Northeast," 40.

47. Pope Francis, Apostolic Exhortation *Evangelium Gaudium* (November 24, 2013), no. 27, http://w2.vatican.va/content/francesco/en/apost_exhortations/documents/papa-francesco_esortazione-ap_20131124_evangelii-gaudium.html.

6

Ministry and Sacramentality in Faith Communities without Resident Priest Pastors

Peter Gilmour

Then I shall go to the altar of God
To the God of my joy,
I shall rejoice, I shall praise you on the harp,
Yahweh, my God.

Why so downcast, my soul,
why do you sigh within me?
Put your hope in God: I shall praise him yet,
My savior, my God.

—Psalm 43:4–5; Jerusalem Bible

Introduction: Two Megatrends

1. Catholicism is developing a pastoral consciousness of a World Church.

2. Catholicism's ministries are increasingly lay centered.

These two megatrends of contemporary Catholicism—World Church and lay centeredness—first emerged from the pastoral experiences of faith communities striving to be authentic to the gospel in their given situations. From those pastoral experiences, theologies were developed that undergirded the Second Vatican Council (1962–65) and the ongoing postconciliar theologies. Karl Rahner makes note of this process:

> I also do not doubt that such happen for the most part and in the final analysis they are not first planned out theologically and then put into effect, but are unreflectively realized through a finally hidden instinct of the Spirit and of grace that remains mysterious—even though the element of reflection borne along with the action should certainly not be disregarded or considered superfluous.[1]

The first megatrend—World Church—is Karl Rahner's description of the present epoch the church finds itself entering. It is a shift away from an institutionalized Eurocentric church to a significantly more diverse church "inculturated throughout the world."[2] This shift, according to Rahner, is as radically boundary breaking as was the shift from Jewish Christianity to Eurocentric Christianity in the early history of the church.

The second megatrend—lay-centered ministries—is obvious in many precincts of American Catholicism as well as other venues of the emerging World Church. The number of laypeople who now hold positions of prominence and service that at one time were the exclusive realm of priests and vowed religious, for example, leadership positions in Catholic parishes, educational institutions, hospitals, retreat houses, dioceses, and even the Vatican, grow by the day.

Laypeople, particularly in parishes, increasingly are involved in ministerial activities once the exclusive realm of the priest. A theology of baptism initiating believers into their right and responsibility to minister undergirds the ever-emerging lay centeredness of Catholicism's ministries.

For nearly a biblical generation now, people other than priests have led parishes without resident priest pastors. These individual and collective experiences are ripe for serious and substantial theological reflection. Theological reflection on people other than priests pastoring parishes will contribute to developing theologies that honor this already existing reality, and illuminate the now and future faith communities, both locally and universally.

In other areas of the world where the structure of national and territorial parishes did not become normative, other forms of Catholicism developed that did not rely on the continual presence of a priest. Theological reflection on these forms of Catholic tradition and practice also will contribute to the developing theologies undergirding World Church.

It is the thesis of this paper that the fruits of such theological reflection focused both on eucharistic celebrations and particularized expressions of popular religious practices are essential to the planning processes of dioceses faced with the challenges of the present and future. While this paper primarily focuses on parishes pastored by people other than priests, it also briefly reflects on other forms of Catholicism not traditionally centered on the frequent celebration of the Eucharist. Latinx[3] ecclesial traditions are singled out as one example of other forms of Catholic faith expression that developed and have been practiced independent of ordained priestly leadership.

The Hidden History of People Other than Priests Who Pastored

The Second Vatican Council and its postconciliar theologies have considerably advanced the understanding of people other than priests who hold ministerial positions within the church. Yet people other than priests, particularly women, have been actively if not officially recognized as ministers within the church from the earliest days of Christianity. Their once hidden history now, through careful research, scholarship, and narrative, has become noticed and notable. Here is one example from research and scholarship:

> In 1915 Thomas Augustine Judge found Mrs. John O'Brien serving as the pastor to the twenty-five Catholics in the tiny mill town of Tallassee, Alabama. When the itinerant pastor came to town each month, he said Mass in Mrs. O'Brien's home. On other Sundays Mrs. O'Brien led her flock in hymns, the rosary, and recitations from the catechism. During Lent she led them in the stations of the cross. "She is a living St. Vincent de Paul Society," Judge affirmed. "When Mrs. O'Brien is seen on the street, the people say: Somebody is sick or dying, there goes Mrs. O'Brien." Women like Mrs. O'Brien, working on their own initiative on the frontiers, prior to the establishment of parish and diocesan programs, were quite literally the pillars and cornerstones of the expanding parish system.[4]

Here is yet another example, a narrative told by the daughter of a woman who pastored a church without a priest pastor:

> My mother, she was the one who was known in the church for "keeping things goin'." I can't tell you how many times I heard people say to me, "Your mama, she's the one that keeps things goin'." And when people used to compliment her on the job she did, she'd humbly beg off, saying that it was nothing, and that she "just kept things a goin'."
>
> My job, I remember, was to walk down to the bus stop every Sunday morning, wait for the bus to come, and escort Father to the church. Being Catholic in that small Oklahoma town in the 1930s was not the most popular thing to be, and to walk down the main street every Sunday with Father all decked out in his Roman Collar probably didn't add much to it. But mama was always so insistent. I had to be there before the bus pulled in to meet him, even though Father certainly knew the way to church.
>
> It wasn't until I heard about this nonordained pastor thing that's come up recently that I finally figured out exactly what mama did all those years back in the Dust Bowl and Depression. Why yes, she was the nonordained pastor of our church, but, of course, back then no one knew what to call her, so they just said, "Your mama, she's the one that keeps things goin'."[5]

These are but two examples of what no doubt are many more illustrative of people other than priests pastoring well before the Second Vatican Council. These stories need to be included in the church's ever-evolving ecclesiology along with the ecclesiology that developed as a result of the Second Vatican Council and the subsequent 1983 Code of Canon Law.

The Role and Function of Canon Law

Canon law regulating the internal management of the Roman Catholic Church is a remarkably tensile body of laws. It is not a rigid rulebook applicable in the same manner to every situation in the thousands of dioceses throughout the world.

Canon law often codifies what has already been established as custom in local church practice. Edward Schillebeeckx makes this point in his book, *Ministry*:

> If we are to evaluate the possible theological significance of present-day new alternatives and forms of ministry which often deviate from the established order of the church, and are on the increase everywhere, we must steep ourselves in the facts of the history of the church: in antiquity, in the Middle Ages and in modern times. It will then also become clear that authoritative documents (the authority of which the Catholic theologian accepts, albeit not always to the same degree) are always prepared for by new practices which arise from the grassroots.[6]

Once codification of custom occurs in canon law, polyvariant interpretations emerge. One reason for varied interpretation is that canon law is filled with provisional language. For example, canon 517 begins, "When circumstances so require." But there is no explanation of these circumstances. Canon 526 reads, "A parish priest is to have the parochial care of one parish only. However, because of a shortage of priests or other circumstances, the care of a number of neighboring parishes can be entrusted to the one parish priest." What the "other circumstances" are and what might be the maximum number of parishes one priest can pastor is not delineated.

Interpretation and application of canon law differ widely among dioceses. Here, in the United States, one diocese might apply certain canons quite differently than another diocese.[7] Some bishops allow nonordained people and permanent deacons to pastor parishes; other bishops do not. In the dioceses that employ people other than priests to pastor parishes without priests, what they are officially allowed to do also varies. Some bishops allow people other than priests or permanent deacons who are pastoring parishes to baptize and witness marriages. Other bishops do not. Some bishops allow people other than priests or permanent deacons to deliver homilies at Mass, which is permitted by canon 766. Other bishops do not.

A change of bishops might change the interpretation and application of canon law for particular dioceses. For example, in the Archdiocese of Chicago, Cardinal Joseph Bernardin appointed people other than priests to pastor parishes; when Cardinal Francis George succeeded him, he abandoned this practice. In other dioceses the reverse has happened. Bishops have extraordinary power to apply various canons within their dioceses as they see fit. There is but one canon law, but multiple interpretations and applications of that single code of church law.

Two Canons Worthy of Note

Embedded within the 1,752 canons, canon 517.2 reads,

> If, because of a shortage of priests, the diocesan Bishop has judged that a deacon, or some other person who is not a priest, or a community of persons, should be entrusted with a share in the exercise of the pastoral care of a parish, he is to appoint some priest who, with the powers and faculties of a parish priest, will direct the pastoral care.[8]

Even though the intentionality of this canon was substantially designed for missionary areas of the world where infrastructures of traditional parishes are often nonexistent,[9] a handful of visionary bishops in the United States saw its potential for staffing already existing parishes in rural dioceses where there were more parishes than priests. This has been the canon upon which an understanding and practice of people other than priests pastoring parishes in the United States of America rests.

Another canon embedded within the 1983 Code of Canon Law, 516.2 reads, "Where some communities cannot be established as parishes or quasi-parishes, the diocesan Bishop is to provide for their spiritual care in some other way." This canon gives bishops a broad spectrum of viable alternative futures, yet it has been ignored by most all dioceses in the United States in favor of canon 517.2. One archdiocese—Poitiers, France—has re-created itself in light of canon 516.2 and will be explored later in this essay.

Pope St. John Paul II, on promulgating the 1983 Code of Canon Law, stressed the importance of interpreting canon law within the contexts of the Gospel and faith:

> Thus the writings of the New Testament enable us to understand still more the importance itself of discipline and make us see better how it is more closely connected with the saving character of the evangelical message itself.
>
> This being so, it appears sufficiently clear that the Code is in no way intended as a substitute for faith, grace and the charisms in the life of the Church and of the faithful. On the contrary, its purpose is rather to create such an order in the ecclesial society that, while assigning the primacy to faith, grace and the charisms, it at the same time renders

easier their organic development in the life both of the ecclesial society and of the individual persons who belong to it.[10]

The Experience of Parishes Pastored by People Other than Priests

In the early 1980s some bishops in rural dioceses of the United States, rather than closing or merging long-existing parishes, decided to appoint personnel other than priests to administer parishes lacking resident priest-pastors. Eventually, this movement spread to certain midsize and large dioceses. In 1985, just two years after the promulgation of the new Code of Canon Law, ninety-three parishes in the United States had parishes led by people other than priests. In 1993, there were 268 parishes led by people other than ordained priests. In 2004, there were 566 of these parishes pastored by people other than priests across the dioceses in the United States.[11]

Initially many parishioners in these parishes who were the recipients of people other than priests leading their faith communities feared it was the diocese's first step to close or merge their parish. However, the repeated behavior pattern in these parishes is that once the parishioners realized ministry continued, sometimes more effectively than past performances of some priest-pastors, most all embraced this model.[12]

This model of parish leadership continues to grow throughout the United States, but with three caveats. First, as already mentioned, a change of bishops in a diocese might well mean a change in policy regarding the appointment of people other than priests to pastor parishes. Second, there has been a decided shift from religious women and laypeople to permanent deacons functioning in this role.[13] Most all of the early appointments of people other than priests to pastor parishes were religious women who were theologically educated, familiar with consensus-oriented decision-making in their respective religious orders, and employed this style of leadership in their newly found role leading faith communities. Third, though "non-ordained pastors" was the most highly descriptive and communicative phrase that captured the reality of their presence and ministry, the appointment of permanent deacons to pastor parishes has rendered this description inaccurate since they are ordained. The term "pastoral administrators" is now commonly used to identify people who function in this role.

Responses to the Reality of People Other than Priests Pastoring Parishes

As has been suggested, there is an accumulated wealth of experience from the reality of people other than priests pastoring parishes ripe for study, for theological reflection, and for further development of theologies undergirding this precinct of World Church. Four dimensions useful to understand and reflect on this experience have emerged: (1) substitution, (2) reconfiguration, (3) ministry, and (4) sacramentality.

Substitution

Substitution is the most immediate response to lack of a priest to pastor a parish. This response is predicated on someone temporarily missing from an existing position, and a replacement is needed for a short time. Day-to-day functions continue, but any kind of change in basic orientation or long-range planning is delayed until the time when the missing person returns or a permanent

Creativity in Church Management: Entrepreneurship for a 21st-Century Parish

replacement is eventually named. Substitution has been focused on individual parishes on a case-by-case basis.

The appointment of people other than priests to pastor parishes benefits already existing faith communities by maintaining their singular heritage and identity, their church buildings along with other physical structures, and their pastoral services and programs, except for the celebration of reconciliation, the Eucharist on weekdays, and sometimes funeral and nuptial Masses. Most Sundays a visiting priest leads the Eucharist. But in the future that could become less frequent depending on the number of priests who are available to preside at Sunday Eucharists.

Reconfiguration

Reconfiguration, unlike substitution, takes a diocesan-wide perspective rather than a parish-by-parish focus. On this level, diocesan officials look at the present and projected availability of their priests and the number of priests that are now needed and will be needed to pastor their parishes. Dioceses then implement a series of decisions that bring the number of parishes in congruence with the number of available priests to pastor them. Closing small parishes, merging nearby parishes, and creating megaparishes are various strategies employed to reconfigure dioceses. Some dioceses have become reconfigured almost overnight to the surprise of many. For example, the Diocese of Essen, Germany, went from nearly 270 parishes to 43 parishes almost overnight in 2005.[14] Other dioceses have moved more slowly. The Archdiocese of Chicago announced a gradual reconfiguration process that will extend over a projected ten-year period and is estimated to close at least 25 percent of existing parishes.[15] The imperatives of this initiative titled "Renew My Church" "will be brought to life by new plans, programs, efforts, and material focused on: Evangelization and Formation, Vocations, Leadership Development and Support, Parish Mission Vitality, School Mission Vitality, Faith in Action, and Society Engagement."[16]

Both the substitution and reconfiguration strategies are essentially transactional. They are primarily focused on preserving semblances of institutional structures as they already exist. The substitution model gives people other than priests an opportunity to engage in significant pastoral responsibilities. The reconfiguration model often eliminates the need for people other than priests to pastor parishes since the number of parishes is lessened. The substitution model preserves already existing faith communities. The reconfiguration model creates new, larger entities, often at the expense of already existing, albeit smaller, faith communities.

What often appears lacking in these two approaches are theological perspectives. It is in these next two approaches that theological perspectives become more apparent.

Ministry

The theology of ministry that has been made explicit by the Second Vatican Council and postconciliar theologies flow from an understanding of church as the people of God and an understanding of ministry flowing from baptism. A parish is a particular faith community essentially consisting of a group of baptized Christians ministering to one another and to others outside their own faith community.

This theology of ministry transcends the pre–Vatican II concept that only priests minister to those who are not priests, that is, parishioners. It deemphasizes a hierarchical structure symbolized by a steeply pitched triangle with pope, bishops, and priests at the top, and laypeople underneath in favor of a significantly less pitched hierarchical communion.

This response from contemporary understandings of church and ministry is a recognition and empowerment of ministering faith communities vital to the present and essential for the future of the church. It does not appear that something or some person is momentarily missing and needs to be temporarily replaced as does the substitution model proffer. Nor does it need to eliminate already existing faith communities as is often the result of the reconfiguration model approach.

A specific example of a diocese that has embraced a response from ministry is the Archdiocese of Poitiers, France, located about two hundred miles southwest of Paris. Instead of following canon 517.2, which allows the substitution of priest pastors with religious women, deacons, or lay ministers, the diocese inaugurated a participative synodal process that embraced canon 516.2. This canon allows a bishop to develop other ways of organizing a diocese when traditional parish structures can no longer function. The archdiocese was divided into "pastoral sectors," each with a pastoral council responsible for the proclamation of the Gospel, prayer, and service, in addition to the financial management of the sector. Additionally, they are responsible for renewing membership of the sector's pastoral council newly elected members every third year.

This model challenges the viability of traditional parishes and the long-entrenched clerical model of leadership. "One world is being erased and another is emerging, without there being any predetermined model for its construction," wrote the French bishops in their 1996 letter. In the Archdiocese of Poitiers, centralization and reproductive change were abandoned for a new way of doing things, that is, decentralization and productive change. The bishop is the pastor of every sector. This experiment, launched about twenty-five years ago, is still considered to be in an early stage of development even though other dioceses have emulated parts of this plan.[17]

The experiment of the Archdiocese of Poitiers is similar to what Marshall McLuhan calls a breakboundary. The previous way of doing things, that is, the traditional parish with a resident priest pastor, cannot be a useful template for this new way of organizing pastoral presence and services across a diocese. Rather, a ministering faith community responsible for its present and its future has become authoritative and normative in this particular archdiocese.

Sacramentality

"More than 90% of the non-ordained pastors interviewed in 2005 saw themselves as the quotidian pastoral and spiritual leader of their parish."[18] Yet they are institutionally prevented from presiding at Eucharist, offering absolution at reconciliation rites, and administering the anointing of the sick because they are not ordained to priesthood. Other sacraments traditionally reserved for priests and permanent deacons—baptisms and weddings—may be done by people other than priests if their local bishops permit. Most bishops in the United States do not permit people other than priests or permanent deacons to preside at baptisms and weddings.

Two rites that people other than priests do preside at that have been developed for use with local faith communities who do not have a priest available for Mass are (1) "Rite for Distributing Holy Communion Outside Mass" and (2) "Sunday Celebrations in the Absence of a Priest."[19] In the United States, the weekday rite conducted by people other than priests is much more common than the Sunday celebration in the absence of a priest. Most parishes pastored by people other than priests in the United States still have priests available for Sunday liturgy.

These rituals have led to two responses, one from members of local faith communities who experience these services, the other from the National Federation of Priests' Councils (NFPC). These two responses reside at opposite ends of the theological spectrum. The trope, "I like Sister's Mass more than the visiting priest's Mass" well captures the reaction to these rites by many churchgoing Catholics living in parishes no longer having resident priest pastors. They experience these rites as an alternate form of Eucharist. On the other hand, the NFPC introduced the word, "eucharist-less" into the theological lexicon in a 1991 report to describe a parish without a priest-led liturgy.[20]

Are faith communities pastored by people other than priests eucharistic or eucharist-less? Can a community of faith without the presence of an ordained priest be eucharistic? Traditional Catholic theology deems the action of an ordained priest essential to the celebration of the Eucharist. However, the hermeneutics of experience, that is, "Simply put, we need to develop the capacity to see it as it is and so be able to tell it as it is."[21] The hermeneutics of experience suggest a different understanding of constitutive elements of a eucharistic community of faith.

Few if any Catholics would argue with the centrality of sacraments, primarily the Eucharist, in the tradition of their church. Rooted in the scriptural narratives in ways no other sacrament is, Eucharist is the epicenter of the church. Celebrations of the Eucharist certainly predate the emergence of a highly pitched hierarchical structure, and, in all probability, the development of a priesthood characterized by exclusive power to consecrate bread and wine.

Yet, given the centrality of Eucharist in the tradition, the nearly two millennium history of its celebration is extraordinarily diverse. A eucharistic meal celebrated in an early house church, Eucharist celebrated in times of persecution on martyrs' graves in catacombs, elaborate cathedral celebrations of the Eucharist akin to the pageantry of medieval royal households, and the "noble simplicity" motif of the Second Vatican Council's Constitution on the Sacred Liturgy (no. 34) differ from one another greatly. Participants from one era might have difficulty recognizing the celebration of the Eucharist as practiced in another era.

Does the definition of what is Eucharist, and, conversely, what is eucharist-less, reside totally and completely on the presence of an ordained priest? Might Eucharist be connected existentially with communities of faith, ritually with the authority of the local community, and institutionally with the wider universal church, that is, the World Church?

There are many ways to be eucharistic, not just one way. In the pre–Vatican II church, visits to the Blessed Sacrament as well as receiving communion outside of Mass were encouraged. Benediction was almost always included as part of novenas and missions. The Forty Hours Devotion was an annual event in most all parishes. These Eucharistic practices were based on a theology that stressed Eucharist as object rather than as a communal celebration reenacting the Last Supper. Nonetheless, they were powerful sacramental rites in the life of the pre–Vatican II church.

Might the various rites and settings of other sacraments suggest there is more than one way to celebrate Eucharist? The styles and rites of baptism, reconciliation, and the anointing of the sick vary depending upon the situation. The rite for infant baptism differs from an adult baptism at the Easter Vigil; there are multiple rites for reconciliation; and the rites for the anointing of the sick vary, depending on whether it is celebrated at the scene of an accident or at a parish communal rite in church. Additionally, it is important to note that anyone can baptize in case of an emergency. Couples confer the sacrament of matrimony on each other; the priest or other designated minister functions only as witness to this sacrament. Sacraments, their history, their rites, their administration, are far more diverse than uniform. Why then are communities of faith totally dependent on an ordained priest to celebrate their eucharistic identity?

Might the aforementioned rites of weekday and Sunday celebrations in the absence of a priest be considered alternate ritual forms of Eucharist much the same way other sacraments have alternate ritual forms? Might the many and varied eucharistic practices throughout the history of Christianity be creatively reconfigured in such a way to keep Eucharist central to the practice of Catholicism and reflect a contemporary understanding of Eucharist as communal thanksgiving reflecting the Lord's Supper?

Of course, the above suggestions are predicated on the continuance of an exclusively male, celibate clergy and the existence of parishes that at one time served well European and United States Catholicism. If the past is an accurate prediction of future behavior, then there is little likelihood of priestly ordination being significantly expanded throughout the world to include women, married or single, and married men. Likewise, there is little concern about the parish as an institutional entity going out of existence, although parishes will, in all probability, be fewer in number and greater in size. Without an expansion of possible candidates for the priesthood, the church will need to search for means other than the celebration of the Eucharist by an ordained priest to ensure the centrality of the Eucharist within the Roman Catholic tradition.

Other Focal Points of Faithfulness

There are, of course, other traditions within Catholicism not exclusively centered on the Eucharist that have been extraordinarily generative for local church communities. The Latinx church, which has become a significant dimension of United States' Catholicism, is one such place that, for various reasons, houses traditions that do not necessarily rely on the presence of priests. Natalia Imperatori-Lee, in her book *Cuentame*, relates the reality of Catholicism's continuance in a church with few clergy:

> *It may be impossible to discern whether U.S. Latinx Catholicism features so much nonliturgical piety because of the relative lack of clergy in Latin American history or because of the Iberian Catholic roots of this region. Iberian Catholicism emphasized local devotions and deemphasized parish life, rendering clergy less important and therefore fostering the flourishing of extraparochial practices. In either case, the relationship between a lack of native clergy in Latin America and the blossoming of popular religion that exists on the periphery of parish life and/or in homes is symbiotic. If there are not enough priests because you live in a rural area, or if the priests are all Spaniards or criollos and you are indigenous or mestizo/a, maybe they don't fully understand you culturally. Maybe the clergy is aligned with a colonial government or oligarchy that oppresses you. In either scenario, if the priest doesn't "get" you, you might supplement worship and spirituality with devotions at home or somewhere else outside the official parish. If the Catholic DNA in Latin American, Iberian Catholicism, already included a propensity to favor local devotions and not parish life, then this tendency makes all the more sense.[22]*

Knowledge of, appreciation for, and encouragement of these "extraparochial practices" not solely reliant on priests could well be constitutive elements of the evolving World Church Karl Rahner envisions.

Conclusion

The fourfold dimensions of this paper that examine changing parish life are not intended to be understood as separated and unrelated. All four dimensions—substitution, reconfiguration, ministry, and sacramentality—are present at various times and degrees in the ever-ongoing process of ensuring Christ's presence in the world through the structures and ministries of the church.

Personnel get sick, die, or need to be removed for cause, and substitutes fill positions suddenly left vacant as a temporary measure. Contemporary situations, for example, decline in church attendance, cathedral-sized churches serving chapel-sized congregations, migration patterns of world populations, the decline in the number of available priests, and lack of finances are but some of the factors motivating reconfiguration of dioceses. These two dimensions, necessary and needed in many existential situations dioceses today find themselves facing, if implemented without an equal attention paid to ministry and sacramentality, are inadequate. Substitution and reconfiguration alone prop up external structures at the expense of the inner dynamism of faith communities.

These last two dimensions—ministry and sacramentality—need attention equal to what has been given to substitution and reconfiguration as dioceses deal with the present and face the future. There is no lack of laypeople who are interested in ministry. Thousands upon thousands have attended university-based schools of ministry in Catholic universities through the United States of America and hold graduate degrees in divinity, pastoral studies, pastoral counseling, and in other allied fields. Many others have participated in substantial diocesan programs of lay ministry. This educated cadre of people is responsible for a great deal of pastoring in parishes throughout the United States and in other parts of the world. The theology of ministry and its practice by a much wider pool of people other than priests has been one of the significant developments in Catholic life and practice contributing to the lay centeredness of the World Church. The Archdiocese of Poitiers, France, for example, stands today as an impressive example of a serious and substantial response from ministry building on lay-centeredness.

But the structured parish and the frequent celebration of sacraments are not the only ways in which Catholicism has thrived as evidenced by the Latinx church. There are other ways the church has survived and thrived in other parts of the world: home-based rituals, local devotions, base communities, pilgrimages, street processions, shine visitation, and other sacramental practices that are not necessarily centered on the presence of a priest. Might the experience of the Latinx church with its emphasis on sacramental practices point to a pastoral charism independent of priestly leadership that might be a future for regions of the world now experiencing a decline in the number of priests? The World Church respects and encourages the many and varied ways the faithful have found to express their Catholicism. Diversity, not uniformity is the charism of the coming World Church.

The nascent World Church continues to mature, in good part through the ministries of its participants. "[Their ministries] are not first planned out theologically and then put into effect, but are unreflectively realized through a finally hidden instinct of the Spirit and of grace that remains mysterious—even though the element of reflection borne along with the action should certainly not be disregarded or considered superfluous."[23]

Catholicism's future will be achieved through courage and creativity throughout the many and varied precincts of the World Church. The particular ministry of people other than priests pastoring faith communities is one such ministry that has become explicit this past generation. Such a ministry calls for a courageous and creative sacramentality to undergird and sustain faith communities led by people other than priests. Likewise, the many and varied practices of faithful Catholics around the world not specifically centered on parish structures and the presence of an ordained priest that undergird and sustain faith communities are yet other constitutive dimension of Catholicism's future incarnated in the coming World Church.

> I wash my hands in innocence
> And join the procession round your altar,
> Singing a hymn of thanksgiving,
> Proclaiming all your wonders.
> I love the house where you live,
> The place where your glory makes its home.
>
> ...I bless you, Yahweh, at the Assemblies.

—Psalm 26: 6–8, 12; Jerusalem Bible

Notes

1. Karl Rahner, "Toward a Fundamental Theological Interpretation of Vatican II," *Theological Studies* 40 (December 1979): 723.

2. Rahner, "Toward a Fundamental Theological Interpretation of Vatican II," 718.

3. "In an effort to be as inclusive as possible, some scholars have adopted the use of the letter 'x' in place of the masculine- or feminine-gendered nouns in Spanish, substituting, for example *hermanxs* for *hermanos/as*." Natalia Imperatori-Lee, *Cuentame: Narrative in the Ecclesial Present* (Maryknoll, NY: Orbis Books, 2018), xxii–xxiii.

4. Jay Patrick Dolan, ed., *Transforming Parish Ministry* (New York: Crossroad, 1989), 220.

5. This testimony was related to me by a woman and I wrote it down afterward, trying to capture what she said and how she said it.

6. Edward Schillebeeckx, *Ministry: Leadership in the Community of Jesus Christ* (New York: Crossroad, 1981), 3.

7. James A. Coriden, "Parish Pastoral Leaders: Canonical Structures and Practical Questions," *The Jurist* 67 (2007): 462.

8. Quotes from the Code of Canon Law are from Canon Law Society of Great Britain and Ireland et al., *The Code of Canon Law in English Translation* (Grand Rapids, MI: Eerdmans, 1983).

9. Ruth A. Wallace, *They Call Her Pastor: A New Role for Catholic Women* (Albany: State University of New York Press, 1992), 7–8.

10. John Paul II, Apostolic Constitution *Sacrae Disciplinae Leges* for the Promulgation of the New Code of Canon Law, January 25, 1983, http://w2.vatican.va/content/john-paul-ii/en/apost _constitutions/documents/hf_jp-ii_apc_25011983_sacrae-disciplinae-leges.html.

11. CARA (Center for Applied Research in the Apostolate), Special Report: "Understanding the Ministry and Experience: Parish Life Coordinators in the United States" (Summer 2005) (Washington, DC: Georgetown University), 1.

12. Peter Gilmour, *The Emerging Pastor: Catholic Non-Ordained Pastors* (Kansas City: Sheed and Ward, 1986), 90–91.

13. CARA, *Word, Liturgy, Charity: The Diaconate in the U.S. Catholic Church, 1968–2018* (Lanham, MD: Lexington Books, 2018), 39.

14. See "A Crisis of Trust, a Crisis of Credibility, a Crisis of Leadership: The Catholic Church in Germany in Quest of New Models," in *Collaborative Parish Leadership: Contexts, Models, Theology*, ed. William A. Clark and Daniel Gast (Lanham: MD: Lexington Books, 2017), 141–54.

15. For the thinking of the Archbishop of Chicago undergirding this initiative, see Cardinal Blase J. Cupich's afterword, "The Chicago Experience of 'Renew My Church,'" in Louis. J. Cameli, *Church, Faith, Future: What We Face, What We Can Do* (Collegeville, MN: Liturgical Press, 2017), 95–104.

16. Archdiocese of Chicago, *Renew My Church: Called by Jesus Christ, We Are Making Disciples, Building Communities and Inspiring Witness* (Chicago: Archdiocese of Chicago, 2017), 1.

17. See "The Local Communities of Poitiers: Reflections on Their Reflections," in Clark and Gast, *Collaborative Parish Leadership*, 155–74, for more details on this innovative diocesan restructuring.

18. Kathy Hendricks, *Parish Life Coordinators: Profiles of an Emerging Ministry* (Chicago: Loyola Press, 2009), 20.

19. United States Conference of Catholic Bishops, Bishop's Committee on the Liturgy, *Sunday Celebrations in the Absence of a Priest*, bilingual ed. (Washington, DC: United States Conference of Catholic Bishops, 2007).

20. National Federation of Priests' Councils, *Priestless Parishes: Priests' Perspective* (Washington, DC: National Federation of Priests' Councils, 1991), 11.

21. Bernard J. Cooke, *Sacraments and Sacramentality* (Mystic, CT: Twenty-Third Publications, 1983), 31, 32.

22. Natalia Imperatori-Lee, *Cuéntame: Narrative in the Ecclesial Present* (Maryknoll, NY: Orbis Books, 2018), 109.

23. Rahner, "Toward a Fundamental Theological Interpretation of Vatican II," 723.

7

New Metrics and Processes for Evaluating Parish Consolidations

Mark Mogilka

National Perspective

Since 2005, more than 10 percent of all existing parishes in the United States have been created or exist through a consolidation or merger of two or more parishes. It is anticipated that the number of consolidated parishes will grow in the future. The reasons for this trend include population movement, loss of parish income, decline in the number of priests available, fewer number of parishes, and a rise in the number of parishes without a priest. These trends are especially prominent in the midwestern and northeastern parts of the United States (Zech et al. 2017).

As an indicator of future trends, during 2018, several dioceses announced plans for future parish reorganizations and consolidations. They include but are not limited to the following:

- Diocese of Pittsburgh: plans to merge 188 existing parishes into 48 by 2025
- Archdiocese of Hartford: plans to go from 212 parishes to 85 pastorates by 2027 (it should be noted that a pastorate is not a consolidated new canonical parish, but does involve consolidation of many parish functions within the pastorate)
- Archdiocese of Chicago: plans to close 100 parishes in the next twelve years
- Diocese of Trier, Germany: will transition from 172 parishes to 35 by 2020

In the *Emerging Models of Pastoral Leadership Project*, utilizing research conducted by CARA (Center for Applied Research in the Apostolate) in 2011, in one part of the study, a wide sampling of *parishioners* from throughout the United States were asked to evaluate the following aspects of parish life (Gray 2012):

- Ministry of pastor
- Sacramental preparation
- Children's religious education
- Marriage preparation
- Youth ministry
- Vision provided by pastor
- Parish pastoral council
- Bible study

- Retreats
- Parishioner faith education

When comparing evaluations from parishioners from traditional parishes, that is, those that had one pastor and have not been consolidated since 2005, to parishioners from consolidated parishes, on average, parishioners from traditional parishes ranked these items as excellent an average of nine percentage points higher than parishioners whose parish had been through a consolidation. While there was significant difference in the two, the rankings for those from consolidated parishes was still very high for most items.

In this same research project, in another part of the study, *parish leaders* from traditional and consolidated parishes were asked to evaluate a somewhat similar list of parish variables. They included the following:

- Finances
- Recruitment and retention of ministers and staff
- Communicating with parishioners
- Faith education
- Social activities
- Ministry opportunities
- Listening to parishioners
- Welcoming persons with disabilities
- Using councils and committees
- Ministry to elderly
- Ministry to families
- Ministry to grieving
- Ministry to those in financial need
- Cultural/ethnic
- Collaboration with other parishes
- Mass offered in preferred languages
- Celebrating cultural diversity
- Ministry to young adults
- Outreach to inactive Catholics
- Ministry to recent immigrants

Here for the most part, traditional parish leader evaluations, as compared to consolidated parish leader evaluations, provided no statistically significant differences in their rankings. There were however, two noteworthy exceptions. First, leaders in traditional parishes judged that they were better at recruiting and retaining ministers and staff compared to leaders in consolidated parishes. The second significant difference was the evaluation from leaders of consolidated parishes who noted that they were better at outreach to inactive Catholics (Gray 2012).

In business journals and literature on organizational mergers and acquisitions, it is commonly held that most mergers fail from 50 to 80 percent of the time. Failure is defined as loss of employees and profitability, and the inability of the "new" organization to function effectively and efficiently. When merged organizations are studied to determine why the merger failed, two reasons most often cited are (1) lack of employee engagement and (2) failure to address cultural differences among the previously independent organizations (Tomberlin and Bird 2012, Zech and Miller 2008). The implications for parish consolidations is significant. Lack of parishioner engagement and the insensitivity or disregard for the unique cultural differences between parish communities in a merger process can and often does lead to failure.

Case Study

In 2000, a place we'll call "Smithville," with a population just over thirty thousand, had six active Catholic churches located within a mile and a half of the center of the city. Together the parishes shared a Catholic grade school, a high school, and a children's faith formation program. While each parish operated separately, conversations began with pastors and pastoral council members to explore additional ways in which the parishes could cooperate and collaborate with one another.

In 2004, five priests served the six parishes. One pastor served two parishes. According to priest availability projections by the diocese, only three priests would be available to serve the city in the next three to five years. Five of the six parishes had significant annual operating deficits. The deficits and an aging population led to a growing concern for the ability of the parishes to continue to subsidize the shared citywide education programs. Several church buildings and facilities also needed repairs. An interparish planning committee was established to create a long-range strategic pastoral plan for the Catholic community in the city of Smithville.

As the result of an eighteen-month period of planning using an open, transparent, collaborative, fact-based, and data-driven process, the planning committee recommended consolidating all six parishes into one that would have three worship sites. The plan also recommended the appointment of one pastor, two parochial vicars, and a lay staff housed together at a neutral site. The proposed plan was presented to parishioners for their approval, and eventually to the diocese, which endorsed the plan's implementation.

On July 1, 2005, the six parishes of Smithville were consolidated to create St. Mary parish. The consolidated parish had about four thousand households. A new pastor and two parochial vicars were appointed. While parish leaders had to navigate several challenges, for the most part the plan was successfully implemented. As a result of sharing resources, a reduction in churches and facilities, and operating cost savings, deficits were eliminated. A central office was created. A stronger, well-formed team was assembled, and many parish programs and services improved. Finally, financial support for the educational system stabilized.

Assessment and Planning

In early 2016, roughly ten years after the creation of St. Mary, several questions arose regarding the parish. Among the questions being asked both at the parish and by some diocesan officials were the following:

- St. Mary is the largest parish in the diocese with four thousand households. Does it really make sense to have such a relatively large parish? Instead might two or three smaller parishes better serve the Catholic community in Smithville?

- While income during the past several years had been stable, it was not keeping up with inflation. How could this be addressed? Several of the churches and buildings from the former parishes had been closed and disposed of. However, some believed that there were still more buildings than were needed to support the mission and ministries of St. Mary.

- Mass attendance and sacramental reception levels were down. How did this compare to diocese-wide data? Could this be addressed? Some suggested that the consolidation of the parishes was the "worst thing to ever happen" to the Catholic community in Smithville. Was this true? What metrics could be used to determine this?

- Some wondered what degree of unity had been achieved by the parish. Some maintained that instead of being one parish, St. Mary was a kind of federation of separate communities that cooperated with one another on some efforts. How could this be measured?

- The diocesan bishop wished to embrace a vision of church in accord with the call to a "New Evangelization." What did the parish do well in this regard and where might there be room for improvement?

In 2016, an assessment was designed by a parish pastoral planning committee that included the pastor and parish leaders. A member of the diocesan staff with expertise in parish assessment and pastoral planning worked closely with the parish committee. The assessment included the following four key elements:

- One-on-One Leadership Interviews: Twenty-four confidential interviews, using a committee-developed template, were conducted by the diocesan staff member working with the assessment process. These interviews included the pastor, priests, deacons, all full-time paid parish staff members, parish trustees, chairpersons of the pastoral council, finance council, and other key parish leaders as recommended by the pastor and members of the planning committee. These interviews were held in November of 2016 (see appendix A for the template).

- Data Mining: Members of the parish planning committee gathered a wide variety of facts, reports, and data on the parish. Information came both from parish records as well as data annually gathered by the diocese. This included Mass attendance statistics, sacramental participation, facility assessments, and historical financial data. The planning committee also asked each major parish organization to submit a brief report on their activities and suggestions for future planning. Data mining was ongoing throughout the assessment and planning process.

- Parishioner-in-Pew Survey: With the assistance of the diocesan staff, an in-pew survey was done at all the Masses one weekend. The survey consisted of forty mostly ranking or check-mark questions so it could be completed in a short period of time between Masses. The survey was done in January 2017 (see appendix B).

- Parish Leadership Summit: Sixty-five people, including the pastor, parish staff, and lay leaders gathered off-site. The Parish Leadership Summit began on a Friday evening and concluded Saturday afternoon. Purposes for the summit included to prayerfully review all the information gathered and then to provide recommendations to the parish planning committee for the development of a parish strategic pastoral plan. The summit, facilitated by the diocesan staff person, was held in February 2017.

One-on-One Interviews

One-on-one interviews provided unique insights into the internal operation, leadership, and organizational dynamics of St. Mary. It is believed that other assessment techniques such as parishioner or leadership surveys, town hall meetings, focus groups, or other assessment techniques would not have provided the kind of valuable information gleaned through this process.

The interviews affirmed the benefits gained by the consolidation of the parishes. These included cost savings and improved quality of staff, programs, and services. The staff were found to be dedicated and hardworking. There was practically no one on the staff or among lay leaders interviewed who spoke in favor of exploring the feasibility of undoing the consolidation of the parishes, thereby creating two or three smaller parishes to serve the Catholic community as had been suggested.

Areas of concern included an awareness that the pastor was a dynamic, personable, and well-loved man, who provided excellent pastoral care. However, the leadership noted that he could use additional help in the administration of the parish, coordination, and supervision of the staff. There were also concerns regarding building maintenance and costs. This included the belief that there were more buildings than were needed. Leaders were aware of lingering feelings expressed by some parishioners that "things were better" before the consolidation of the parishes. Leaders also expressed concern over tightening budgets and raised concern for the long-term fiscal health of the parish.

Recommendations for the future included getting help for the pastor in the administration of the parish. If resources could be found, leaders recommended the building of one worship site and one school at a common site in the city. Those interviewed also recommended the maintenance of the existing basic staff and organizational structure to serve the Catholic community in Smithville.

Data Mining (Metrics)

Statistics, data, and information or metrics from the parish and diocesan offices was gathered. This included information archived from the previous six parishes in Smithville. Annual reports and information gathered from before and after the founding of St. Mary parish on July 1, 2005, was also gathered. The information included:

- Census data
- Mass attendance, sacramental, parish membership, and education data
- Fiscal reports
- Review of all facilities
- Reports from all parish organizations and ministries
    - Each was asked to submit a three-to-five-page document outlining:
    The purpose of the group
    Their key accomplishments over the past year
    Hopes and dreams for the committee in the future
    A list of hopes and dreams for the parish in the future
    - Parish organization and ministry reports were secured from:
    Pastoral and finance councils
    Worship committee and ministries
    Pastoral and social concerns committees and ministries
    Educational boards and committees

Longitudinal Data Collection

In the case study for St. Mary parish, longitudinal data for nine years prior to the merger and ten years following the merger were gathered and graphed to gauge the potential impact the consolidation may have had on Mass attendance, sacramental participation, and overall financial contributions.

Figure 1 shows Mass attendance data for nineteen years. The merger of the parishes took place on July 1, 2005 (note the line at the center of each graph). The numbers of people attending Mass on weekends prior to 2005 was based on the combined totals of Mass attendance at the six individual churches and parishes. The numbers from 2006 through 2015 are based on the consolidated St. Mary parish with Masses each weekend at three different church buildings. If only data from the beginning of the consolidation were used, it would suggest that one of the impacts of the merger was the gradual decrease in Mass attendance. When using longitudinal data, however, it is obvious that, from 1996 to 2015, the decrease in attendance was part of a trend that goes back at least twenty years. Hence the data suggests that the merger did not cause significant drops in Mass attendance. In fact, comparing this trend to parishes throughout the Diocese of Green Bay, the trend here is similar to overall diocesan-wide trends. It is also like other diocesan Mass attendance trends throughout the midwestern part of the United States. It is also important to note that according to census data, between 2000 and 2016 there was a 3.6 percent drop in the overall population of Smithville, which provides another explanation for the noted consistent decrease in Mass attendance.

FIGURE 1

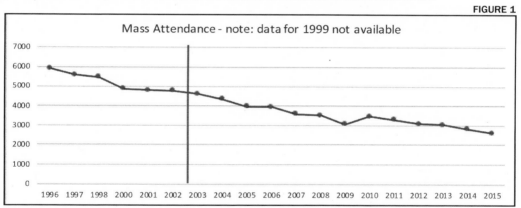

Figure 2 graphs baptisms and Figure 3, marriages. Again, there were no significant trend deviations based on pre- and post-merger data.

FIGURE 2

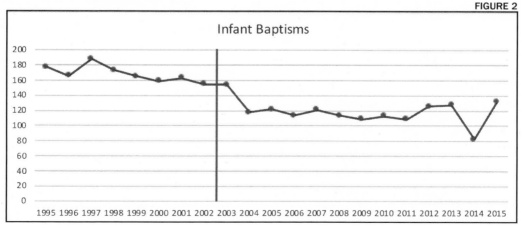

FIGURE 3

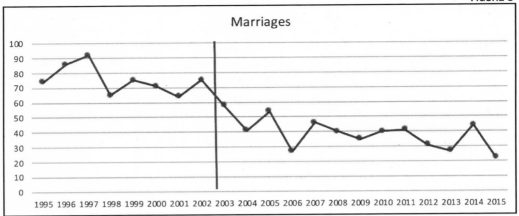

Marriages

Figure 4 presents data concerning overall total parish financial contributions. Figure 5 graphs the number of "contributing units." In the Diocese of Green Bay, contributing units are measured and annually reported. Contributing units are the number of households in the parish that have contributed $100.00 or more over the past year. Again, the impact of the consolidation appears to be negligible in terms of impact on total income and number of contributing households.

FIGURE 4

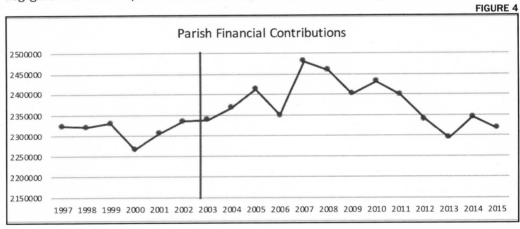

Parish Financial Contributions

FIGURE 5

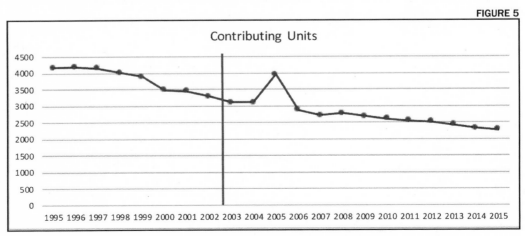

Contributing Units

In-Pew Survey

One weekend, before all the Masses at St. Mary, copies of a forty-question survey were distributed to parishioners. Average weekend Mass attendance, including children and youth was about 2,500; 1,087 surveys were completed and returned for collating. The survey included thirty-four statements about the parish to which parishioners were asked to rank their reactions on a scale of one to five, with one indicating that they strongly disagreed with the statement and five indicating that they strongly agreed with the statement. The instructions also noted that if the respondent did not know or was unsure, they should feel free to leave the item blank. The average score across the thirty-four statements was 3.9 with a range of 2.7 to 4.3 (see appendix B for the survey).

Overall, parishioners ranked the parish positively as shown by the following highly ranked statements. It is interesting to note the significant number of respondents who were unable to provide rankings for the grade or high school.

	Average Score	Times Left Blank
Overall, the celebration of the Mass each weekend is very good.	4.3	10
Homilies by the priests are engaging and uplifting.	4.3	18
Overall, the pastor is very good.	4.3	29
Overall, the staff is very good.	4.3	38
The Catholic grade school is very good.	4.2	172
The high school is very good.	4.2	170
At St. Mary, members of the parish have ample opportunities to use their gifts and talents.	4.2	47
There are excellent opportunities for laypeople to share in parish leadership.	4.1	58
I know what is expected of me to be a member of St. Mary.	4.1	56
Overall, the parish facilities are well maintained and adequate.	4.1	52
Overall, I am satisfied with St. Mary parish.	4.1	28
Among potential areas for concern, based on the rankings are the following:		
In the past year, I have invited someone to be a member of this parish.	2.7	241
The parish does a good job of reaching out to the unchurched and those who have left the church.	3.3	226
If possible, it would be important to build and new K-8 grade school.	3.4	124
The faith formation program for students who do not attend the Catholic school is very good.	3.5	303
Members of the parish are very generous with their money and share sacrificially.	3.5	109
Ministry to and with youth and young adults is well done.	3.7	193
St. Mary does a good job of inviting people to be members of the parish.	3.7	61

	Average Score	**Times Left Blank**
I feel well informed about what is going on in our parish.	3.7	72
Opportunities for seniors and those who are aging is very good.	3.8	164
The parish ministers well to families.	3.8	179

Here, it is noteworthy that, given the desire of the diocesan bishop to promote a spirit of "New Evangelization," the items that received the lowest rankings and where a significant number of parishioners just didn't know or couldn't provide a ranking, were items related to evangelization.

Worship Site Loyalty

Given that the parish has three worship sites, parishioners were asked, "What percentage of the time do you worship at the following sites?"

Church Location	**75–100%**	**50–74%**	**25–49%**	**1–24%**
North Side	52%	11%	11%	27%
South Side	45%	13%	11%	30%
Central	30%	10%	14%	46%

The data suggest high church-site loyalties for the parish churches located on the north and south sides of town. There is modest site loyalty for the church that is more centrally located.

Degree of Perceived Parish Unity

Parishioners were asked, "Since the merger of the six parishes in Smithville to form St. Mary ten years ago, which of the following statements best describes your perception of how the merger has gone?" The percentages of response to each of the statements follows:

We have become one parish that just happens to have three worship sites: 40%

We are one parish that has three communities: 17%

We are three distinct communities that work well together as St. Mary parish: 12%

We are three distinct communities that cooperate on some things: 11%

We are three very separate communities: 4%

I do not know, am unsure, or left blank: 15%

Survey Open-Ended Suggestions

The last statement on the survey was "As we plan for the future of the Catholic Church in the Smithville area, I think it would be important for the parish planning committee to keep in mind... (please complete this sentence)."

In order of priority, parishioners listed the following as items to keep in mind for the planning process:

1. The engagement of youth, young adults, and families

2. Buildings: maintaining, potential renovations and/or replacement especially of the grade school

3. Weekend worship: quality of music, schedules, bring back Life Teen, work on hospitality

4. Concerns for the short- and long-range financial health of the parish

5. Growing number of seniors

Parish Leadership Summit

Modeled after the example of Pope Francis's desire to lead a more consultative and collaborative church using synods, members of the planning committee decided to include a leadership summit as part of the assessment and planning process. In February 2017, parish staff and leadership gathered for a Parish Leadership Summit. Prior to it, those in attendance received a summary report from the one-on-one leadership interviews, highlights from the data mining, and a report from the in-pew survey. The summit's participants were asked to set aside time to prayerfully consider all the information provided and to come to the Parish Leadership Summit with open minds and hearts to work with the pastor, staff, and other parish leaders to help fashion a pastoral plan for the future of the parish. The summit was facilitated by a member of the diocesan staff. The agenda for the Parish Leadership Summit included the following:

- Affirm the strengths of the parish
- Review and recommend an update to the parish mission statement
- Review background information, demographic, financial, facility data, as well as the organizational reports on the past, present, and future hopes and dreams for the parish as gathered and submitted by parish staff from the various organizations of the parish
- Study the diocesan bishop's call for parishes to embrace the "New Evangelization" to become communities of missionary disciples
- Recommend future parish priorities and brainstorm potential action items the parish could consider utilizing in the implementation of the priorities

Toward the end of the Parish Leadership Summit, participants were asked to name items they would recommend as priorities that would help St. Mary to grow numerically and spiritually in the future. Participants were asked to focus on items that would require additional time and talent. Participants were also asked to prayerfully consider all the information shared prior to and through the various small group and large group dialogues. The summit's attendees were advised that the obvious concerns about too many buildings and budget would be addressed by a special committee of the parish planning committee and therefore should not be included in their discernment of priorities. The items generated through the Parish Leadership Summit process are listed below in prioritized order:

1. Family and young people outreach programs and services

2. Engagement of more people through Mass, prayer, ministries, and so on (all forms of engagement)

3. Get a dynamic chief executive officer or parish administrator

4. Further improve the overall quality of worship

5. Strengthen hospitality ministry

Using the data, metrics, and insights from all four elements of the assessment process, the parish planning committee was able to put together a strong strategic pastoral plan for the future of St. Mary.

Concluding Observations

1. To adequately assess a consolidated parish, multiple perspectives, strategies, and new metrics are needed that can listen to leadership, gather longitudinal data, and secure large samplings of parishioner perceptions, hopes, and dreams. These processes should be the foundation on which dialogue and discernment should take place among parish leaders and parishioners as well as with diocesan leaders for the creation of short- and long-range strategic pastoral plans for consolidated parishes.

2. The likelihood of a successful consolidation is greatly enhanced when the planning and assessment process is not rushed, but is transparent, collaborative, and data driven.

3. While parish consolidations can be very challenging, they need not result in the loss of significant numbers of parishioners.

4. The transition from individual parish identities and loyalties to a common single unified new parish identity and loyalty takes many years.

Bibliography

Gray, Mark M. "Special Report: Multi-parish Ministry Findings: An Emerging Model of Pastoral Leadership." *CARA Report, 2012.*

Gray, Mark M., Mary L. Gautier, and Melissa A. Cidade. "The Changing Face of U.S. Catholic Parishes: Emerging Models of Pastoral Leadership." National Association for Lay Ministry, 2011.

Tomberlin, Jim, and Warren Bird. *Better Together: Making Church Mergers Work.* San Francisco: Jossey-Bass, 2012.

Zech, Charles E., Mary L. Gautier, Mark M. Gray, Jonathon L. Wiggins, and Thomas P. Gaunt. *Catholic Parishes of the 21st Century.* New York: Oxford University Press, 2017.

Zech, Charles, and Robert Miller. *Listening to the People of God: Closing, Rebuilding, and Revitalizing Parishes.* Mahwah, NJ: Paulist Press, 2008.

Appendix A

St. Mary Parish Leader Interview Outline

Name _____ Position _____ Date _____

I.   Introductory Comments

    A. Introduce yourself.

    B. Outline purpose of interview—input for 3- to 5-year plan for the parish.

    C. Emphasize confidentiality—general report to pastor and then planning committee members—no specific names or quotes to be used in report.

II.   Questions to Pose

    A. Briefly describe your position and how long you have been in this position.

    B. In your position, what are you proudest of?

    C. If you had more resources—personnel and/or funding—how would you use them to improve service/ministry in your area of concern?

    D. As you look at the parish, what are 2 or 3 of its greatest strengths overall?

    E. As you look at the parish, what are a couple of areas that could use some additional time, talent, and treasure?

    F. Are you aware of the bishop's new vision and mission statements? If so, how do you anticipate that they might impact your position/ministry and/or the ministry of the parish?

    G. It has been 10 years since the merger of the parishes in the city of Smithville to create St. Mary. In general, how do you think the merger has gone—what has been the impact on the people?

    H. Is there anything else that would be important for members of the planning committee to be mindful of as it seeks to create a strategic pastoral plan for the next 10 years?

III.   Concluding Remarks

    A. Say thanks.

    B. Ask the candidate to contact you if he or she has any additional thoughts, ideas, or suggestions.

Appendix B

For each of the following statements, please circle your response on a scale from 1= strongly disagree to 5= strongly agree. If you do not have an opinion, are unsure, or don't know, feel free to leave it blank.

		Strongly Disagree			Strongly Agree	
1.	Overall, the celebration of the Mass each weekend is very good.	1	2	3	4	5
2.	St. Mary parish is warm, welcoming, and hospitable.	1	2	3	4	5
3.	Music at liturgies is uplifting and well done.	1	2	3	4	5
4.	Homilies by the priests are engaging and uplifting.	1	2	3	4	5
5.	Homilies by the deacons are engaging and uplifting.	1	2	3	4	5
6.	I know what is expected of me to be a member of the parish.	1	2	3	4	5
7.	At St. Mary, members of the parish have ample opportunities to use their gifts and talents.	1	2	3	4	5
8.	Small group opportunities are available and there are several options.	1	2	3	4	5
9.	Because of my involvement in the parish, I regularly experience the Holy Spirit.	1	2	3	4	5
10.	St. Mary does a good job of inviting people to be members of the parish.	1	2	3	4	5
11.	Overall, the pastor is very good.	1	2	3	4	5
12.	Overall, the staff is very good.	1	2	3	4	5
13.	There are excellent opportunities for laypeople to share in parish leadership.	1	2	3	4	5
14.	There are adequate opportunities offered to help adults grow spiritually.	1	2	3	4	5
15.	The parish does a good job serving those in need.	1	2	3	4	5
16.	Members of the parish are very generous with their money and share sacrificially.	1	2	3	4	5
17.	The Catholic grade school is very good.	1	2	3	4	5
18.	If possible, it would be important to build a new K-8 Catholic grade school.	1	2	3	4	5

		Strongly Disagree			Strongly Agree	
19.	The faith formation program for students who do not attend the Catholic school is very good.	1	2	3	4	5
20.	The high school is very good.	1	2	3	4	5
21.	Pastoral ministry to the sick, homebound, those in hospitals/nursing homes, the grieving is very good.	1	2	3	4	5
22.	Opportunities for seniors and those who are aging is very good.	1	2	3	4	5
23.	Overall, the parish facilities are well maintained and adequate.	1	2	3	4	5
24.	It is a good idea to refurbish and make use of the remaining closed church.	1	2	3	4	5
25.	Ministry to and with youth and young adults is well done.	1	2	3	4	5
26.	The parish ministers well to families.	1	2	3	4	5
27.	The parish reaches out to the unchurched and those who have left the church.	1	2	3	4	5
28.	I feel well informed about what is going on in our parish.	1	2	3	4	5
29.	St. Mary is a good stewardship parish.	1	2	3	4	5
30.	I know the mission of the parish and I am committed to it.	1	2	3	4	5
31.	Parishioners are invited, involved, and engaged in the programs and ministries of the parish.	1	2	3	4	5
32.	In the past year, I have invited someone to be a member of this parish.	1	2	3	4	5
33.	I spend time in worship or prayer every day.	1	2	3	4	5
34.	Overall, I am satisfied with St. Mary parish.	1	2	3	4	5

What percentage of the time do you worship at the following sites?

_____ North Side Site

_____ Central Site

_____ South Side Site

Since the merger of the six parishes in Smithville to form St. Mary 10 years ago, which of the following six statements best describes your perception on how the merger has gone? (select one of the following)

_____ We have become one parish that just happens to have three worship sites.

_____ We are one parish that has three communities.

_____ We are three distinct communities that work well together as St. Mary parish.

_____ We are three distinct communities that cooperate on some things.

_____ We are three very separate communities.

_____ I do not know or am unsure.

As we plan the future of the Catholic Church in the Smithville area, I think it would be important for the parish planning committee to keep in mind... (please complete the sentence)

_____

_____

_____

_____

_____

I am: Male _____   Female _____

My age is (check one)

_____ 18–25   _____ 46–55

_____ 26–35   _____ 56–65

_____ 36–45   _____ Over 65

I typically attend Mass

_____ at least weekly

_____ 2–3 times per month

_____ once a month

_____ once or twice a year

8

Francis Xavier's Intercultural Principles and Global Entrepreneurship of the Church in the Twenty-First Century

Tobias Schuckert

The Jesuit missionary movement was a global movement in the sixteenth century launched by the most influential Basque Ignatius of Loyola. One of the first Jesuit missionaries who set off for Asia was Francis Xavier (1505–52). Xavier was successful in his ministry in the Portuguese colonies of India and Malacca. Indeed, he was the first Roman Catholic missionary who brought Christianity to Japan.

This list of countries is even more remarkable considering that Francis left Europe on his thirty-fifth birthday in 1541 and reached Goa/India in 1542, which means that he was working inter-culturally for about only ten years. Francis Xavier is characterized as a brave missionary who was able to endure hard circumstances and had an extraordinary gift to adjust in changing situations.[1] Therefore, he is popular among Roman Catholic as well as Protestant missiologists. One German Protestant historian of mission said about him, "Oh, what if he would have been one of us!"[2] It was only a natural choice that Pope Pius XI proclaimed him in 1927 as patron of the Roman Catholic Church's missionary work.[3]

Xavier never wrote a book. The most information we have about him and his intercultural ministries can be concluded from the letters he wrote. This paper builds on Xavier's biography from the German Jesuit Georg Schurhammer[4] and other missiological sources. It starts with an overview of his biography in which a development in his intercultural approach and understanding will become visible. This first part is going to be the foundation for the principles generated from Xavier's life and intercultural ministry in India, Indonesia, and Japan as well as critical reflections on Xavier's apostolic mission that later became stumbling blocks to the church, especially in Japan as discussed in the second part of this study. In that second step, Xavier's intercultural principles will be applied to cross-cultural entrepreneurship of the church[5] in the globalized world of the twenty-first century. In Europe and in North America, the church faces a severe crisis and she needs a new spirit of entrepreneurship in her mission in and to the world. With this statement, it becomes clear that Christians are called to learn from the "cloud of witnesses" that surrounds them (Heb 12:1) of whom Francis Xavier is one.

Brief Biography

Francis was born as Francisco de Jasso y Azpilicueta on April 7, 1506, in the northern Basque region of Spain in Xavier. He was the sixth child of Juan Jassu y Atondo and Maria de Azpilcueta y Aznárez.

Childhood and Youth (1506–25)

In the village close to the castle where Francis was born, only free people lived. They paid no taxes, not even to the king.[6] This must have had a great influence on Francis's approach to officials. He did not hesitate to meet officials or nobility but was always keen to either confront them with their lax morals or ask them for help in the ministry of the church. Moreover, the American scholar of religion Herb Skoglund shows in his analysis of Francis's letters that he was able to use appropriate diplomatic language, even with a sense of humor.[7]

His father, Juan Jasso, was chair of the royal council of Navarra[8] and, therefore, mostly out of town, so Francis was raised by his uncle Martin of Lezaun, as well as by priests who came to his home to teach him Latin and religion, as well as usual elementary subjects. Regarding Latin, language became an issue from the beginning of his life. Basque was his mother tongue, but the language of the area was Spanish. The issue of language later became a significant theme in Francis's ministry as we will see later in this paper.

Francis grew up in the church, so the seasons of the ecclesiastical year played an important role in his early life. He was accustomed to the rituals and faith of the church.

When he was nine years old, Francis's father died and his older brother Miguel took over the family business of farming.[9] His family wanted him to have a military career like most of his relatives,[10] but he wanted to follow in the footsteps of his father, who received a doctorate in 1470. So in 1525, Francis went to Paris and enrolled at the Sorbonne where he met Ignatius of Loyola. Francis never saw his family again.

At the University in Paris (1525–36)

It was a crucial time in Europe. In 1517, the Augustinian Martin Luther launched the Reformation in Germany. At the University of Paris, there were theological discussions on how to relate to the new Protestant faith. John Calvin came to Paris in 1523, and it is very likely that Francis met him.[11] However, the theological faculty of Paris condemned Luther's teachings in a clear and sharp reply after Luther appealed to them.[12]

By that time, Francis was living with several roommates in the Latin Quarter in the Collège Sainte-Barbe, a kind of dorm with a strict, monastic atmosphere. He had to complete his Latin studies to start regular classes in philosophy.

In 1529, Ignatius of Loyola (1491–1556), another Basque, came to Paris. Ignatius's first career was as a soldier, but he was wounded in battle and had to quit the service.[13] Reading lives of saints during his convalescence, Ignatius experienced a spiritual transformation sometime between 1521 and 1522.[14] By the time he came to Paris, he had already acquired a reputation as a pious troublemaker.[15] Ignatius had a charismatic personality and quickly influenced students to confess their sins and attend Mass on Sunday mornings. The university warned him to desist, but he continued. However, after talking to Ignatius about appropriate punishment, the university's head relented.

Ignatius met Francis and gave him financial and spiritual help, such as general confession, weekly confession, and participation in holy communion and daily examination of conscience. Francis was resistant to Ignatius, however, and did not want to follow him like his close friend Pierre Favre did.[16]

Creativity in Church Management: Entrepreneurship for a 21st-Century Parish

Schurhammer's interpretation of this is that Francis still wished to pursue idle ways.[17] But when his mother and sister died, Francis was thrown into a personal crisis, and he decided to follow Ignatius.

In October 1530, after Francis had completed his master's degree, he started to teach philosophy, mainly Aristotle, and became part of the University of Paris faculty. Although he had found a spiritual guide in Ignatius, he was still without peace. His friend Peter Favre wrote, "He was without peace of mind. His studies were simply an end in themselves and not a means to an ultimate goal. As yet the cross of Christ had no great influence upon him, neither at the beginning, nor in the middle, not at the end of his endeavors."[18]

But, as the legend has it, Ignatius was able to break down Francis's doubts and ambitions with the New Testament verse, "For what will it profit them to gain the whole world and forfeit their life?" (Mark 8:36).[19] This event marked Francis's conversion.[20]

Francis tended toward extremism. For example, he sequestered himself for thirty days alone with God, only visited by Ignatius to do spiritual exercises and he took those to the extreme. He punished himself for having participated in track and field games, where he ranked as one of the best at the high jump. He tied his arms and feet with cords and spent two days sitting like this in pain. His companions feared his limbs would have to be amputated.[21]

Together with their spiritual mentor Ignatius, Francis, Favre, and four other friends founded the Society of Jesus in 1534 on the Feast of the Assumption (August 15). They vowed celibacy, the renunciation of all worldly possessions, and to make a journey to Jerusalem, or if this was not possible, to throw themselves at the feet of the pope and serve wherever the church sent them. Later, they added a vow of obedience to one's superior.[22]

Ignatius left Paris in 1535. Francis and the others who remained at the university dedicated themselves to studying theology in preparation for the priesthood and their apostolate. The British theologian and general secretary of the Church Missionary Society, Henry Venn, writes that during this time without direct influence from Ignatius, Francis developed a "more healthy tone of religion" that impacted his service as missionary.[23]

When they started the Society of Jesus, the first members pledged to conduct a pilgrimage to Jerusalem. However, they never reached the Holy Land.

Venice—Rome—Lisbon (1536–41)

Although Francis was offered a habit of a canon regular, he did not accept it and chose the way of poverty. As we will see later, this decision did not hinder his wearing silk when necessary for his apostolic mission in Asia. On November 15, 1536, he left Paris to fulfill his vow to go to Jerusalem. Together with other Jesuits, he left for Venice on foot to go from there to the Holy Land. They never reached Jerusalem. First, it was too cold, and second, they had to go through Protestant territory. This was before the Peace of Augsburg (1555), which effected the principle *cujus regio ejus religio* ("whose realm, his religion," that is, subjects must accept the religion of their ruler), so it was dangerous to travel through areas that considered themselves Protestant. Moreover, they learned it was also too dangerous to go to Palestine, because the Turks had occupied Jerusalem.[24] They stayed in Venice where they took care of the sick.[25]

The failure of his attempt to go to Jerusalem must have been an important experience for him because this was when he first learned that there were territories outside the realms of Roman Catholicism or Christianity where there was no power he could rely on. This became crucial for his apostolic service later in Japan, where he went beyond Christian territories and started his evangelism with the rulers and the Buddhist bonzes instead of the poor.

In 1537, he was ordained a priest in Venice. Ignatius called him to come to Rome to work for him as secretary in 1538, and in 1539, Francis helped Ignatius to develop the Jesuit's rule.[26] In the same year, King John III of Portugal requested missionaries from Pope Paul III for the Portuguese colonies in East India.

This period might be called the time of consolidation in Xavier's life. He became closer to Ignatius as well as getting more acquainted with the politics of the church. He also witnessed the pope's official recognition of the Jesuits in 1540. Prior to this, the Jesuits were being accused of heresy by conservatives inside the church.[27] In 1541, Francis Xavier was appointed as apostolic delegate. On his thirty-fifth birthday, he left Lisbon and Europe, not knowing if he would ever return. The time of intercultural ministry started. It is remarkable the he worked for only about ten years, but this was the period he became famous for.

Xavier's time as missionary can be divided in two major periods. The first period was among previously Christianized people in Portuguese colonies.

First Period: In Portuguese Colonies (1542–49)

Francis left Europe on April 7, 1541. After a brief stay in Mozambique, he reached Goa in India on May 6, 1542. As apostolic nuncio to Asia, he was appointed to assist in the work of converting Indians in the Portuguese colonies to Christianity. Upon his arrival in Goa, he immediately started to work with young children, teaching them the Lord's Prayer and the catechism.[28]

He stayed in Goa for about five months.[29] Goa would become his mission station from which he went back and forth, the Rome of Asia. Altogether he stayed there for about nineteen months. Looking at Francis Xavier's life, one is reminded of the Apostle Paul, who also tended to stay in cities for short times and traveled back and forth.

In September 1542, Francis went to the Fishery Coast in South India to Tamil Nadu. About twenty thousand people had become Christians but demonstrated little understanding of the Catholic faith. They were mainly from the low-caste pearl divers and fishermen who had become Christians under Portuguese rule.[30] Francis started to translate the first principle of Christianity into Tamil with the help of three seminarians and composed a sermon about what it means to be a Christian. This is significant for two reasons. First, it shows that Xavier saw the importance of Tamil, the local language. We will discuss this further in the second part of this essay. Moreover, this activity shows that the Protestant critique that he merely baptized people but did not care about their faith is wrong.[31] It was important to him that the new believers were taught the doctrines of the church.

Wherever he went, he attracted young children by ringing a bell. Children called him *Periya Padre*, "Great Father."[32] He moved farther south to Tuticorin to stay there for four months, where he preached so much and baptized so many that he lost his voice and his arms ached. Thus, he is often displayed in European churches in the act of baptizing an Indian child.

The pain in his arms may have come from the many baptisms, or it was an early symptom of serious sickness. In September 1543, Francis left Tamil Nadu and returned to Goa where he showed a great gift in using politics to advance his work. Since he had been raised as a free man in Spain, he dared to send a letter to the king of Portugal, the political patron of his mission activity. In this letter Francis demanded that the king be generous and use his material wealth for the spiritual needs of the Indians. Francis regarded political powers as means to reach his spiritual goals. For him, kings and rulers were not equal with the church. This worked well as long as he worked in territories governed by Christian rulers. As we will see, it was different when he left the realm of Christianity.

Despite his great success, Francis had no confidence in an Indian church without European leadership. He wrote to Ignatius of Loyola that he saw "no way of perpetuating our Society through the Indians, natives of the land; and that Christianity will last among them for as long as shall last and live we who are here, or those whom you may send from there."[33]

Francis is regarded as one of the first Roman Catholic European missionaries to Asia to practice inculturation. However, during this period of his missionary career he still had a Western mindset that considered European ways of thinking essential to the faith.[34] The American missiologists Stephen Bevans and Roger Schroeder argue that he still followed "the *tabula rasa* perspective—having contempt for Hinduism, Islam and traditional religions."[35] This Eurocentric mindset changed in the years to follow.

In early 1545, Xavier heard rumors that two kings in the Maluku islands had converted from Islam, been baptized, and had asked for missionaries to instruct their people. After a pilgrimage to the tomb of St. Thomas, Xavier sailed to Malacca, in what is now Indonesia and Malaysia, where he stayed until December 1545. He fought hard against the immorality of the Portuguese, with their numerous Malay concubines and slave girls. He succeeded in a kind of reformation of this wealthy city, while trying hard to learn a bit of Malay. Francis's example of a simple, holy, and hardworking life gave him an irresistible power over the hearts of others, even non-Christians.

Bad news from Macassar brought Xavier to the Christian village of Hatiwi on the island of Ambon in February 1546. On Ambon and the other islands of the Moluccas, Xavier visited officials and tried to persuade the Portuguese to give up their vices. He gave religious instruction to many islanders, using eager young boys as his interpreters and catechists. Hearing about the abandoned Christians on Morotai and northern Halrnahera, he sailed to Ternate, where he was liked by Christians and Muslims alike. Francis composed songs telling salvation history, arranged religious instruction courses, and looked after the sick and dying. On his daring journey to Morotai in an open rowboat, he strengthened the Christian villagers and converted many. He promised to send Jesuit priests to these faraway islands. This became the start of the Jesuit Moluccan Mission (1545–1666).

Apparently, this was a time of change in his mindset. Francis observed the scandalous behavior of the Christian colonizers, their greed and failure to protect the people.[36] But still, he moved in territory ruled by Portugal. Like Paul in Acts, who started by going to the Jewish synagogue when he entered a new city,[37] Francis would go to the Portuguese when entering a new place. This was the bridge that helped Francis to reach out to local people. This would soon change. On his way back to India he met a Japanese fugitive named Anjirô[38] (1511–50) who already spoke Portuguese and was eager to learn about the Christian faith. Anjirô expanded Francis's horizon so that his attention turned toward bringing the Christian faith to that nation in the East that was beyond the authority and protection of the Portuguese *Padroado* (patronage).[39]

Second Period: Beyond Portuguese Protection (1549–51)

Francis Xavier returned to Goa and established St. Paul's College, a school for native boys from Africa and Asia. In 1549, he was appointed the first provincial of the Society of Jesus in Goa. Much of his time was taken up with the administration of the college, the installation of Jesuits from Portugal working in India, and voluminous correspondence.

Anjirô was baptized in 1548 together with two other Japanese. He sparked the desire in Francis's heart to evangelize Japan. Even though he himself was not educated, Anjirô opened a new vision for Francis. When Francis saw Anjirô's willingness to learn, he concluded that all Japanese would like that. Between March 1548 and August 1549, Anjirô translated the Gospel of Matthew into Japanese.[40] The Japanese Divine Word missionary Paul Gen Aoyama reports a further occasion when Francis asked Anjirô if he thought that the Japanese would become Christians if he accompanied him to Japan. Anjirô answered that they would not become Christians quickly but would ask many questions. If Francis answered their questions well and lived according to his teaching, the Japanese nobility and the sophisticated people would all become Christians within six months.[41]

Francis decided to leave the Portuguese territories and go to Japan. Together with two priests,[42] Anjirô and two other Japanese, Xavier left Goa on April 15 and landed at Kagoshima on the island of Kyûshû on August 15, 1549. They were welcomed because the local leaders expected the opening of trade with the Portuguese. Francis began to preach and Anjirô interpreted for him, but he did so rather badly because he used Buddhist terminology with the result that Christianity was misinterpreted as another form of Buddhism.[43]

When they landed in Kagoshima, Anjirôs hometown, around one hundred people converted relatively easily. Most of them were members of Anjirô's family. Anjirô then took over and cared for them spiritually.[44]

Coming to Japan, Francis changed his methodology.[45] Realizing the great influence of the *daimyo*, the warlords, Xavier shifted his approach from the poor and the children to the upper classes.

In the winter of 1550, Francis went to Kyoto, the old capital of Japan, to meet the emperor Go-nara and obtain permission to preach in the whole country. His original plan was to meet "the king of the country" and then preach at the universities.[46] The emperor, however, did not receive him. This rejection taught him a lesson, and he realized the need for more cultural sensitivity. The practice of poverty, diligence, and the high level of morality that helped in other places such as Malacca, were not as helpful as he expected. It was more important to be dressed properly, bring gifts, and to be conversant in science and philosophy.

This shift included wearing fine silk rather than ordinary cotton and presenting the local leaders with gifts from Europe.[47] He started discussions with the Buddhist clergy and tried to understand the Japanese attachment to their ancestors. Francis understood the importance of an intensive adjustment to the local culture.[48] He concluded that the Christian mission in East Asia needed to be built on the local cultures.[49]

Francis could not speak Japanese well and relied on Juan Fernandez, who was proficient in the language, and two talented Japanese, Bernard, who accompanied him on his travels throughout Japan, and a half-blind Japanese minstrel, Brother Laurence.[50] Eventually, Xavier was given permission to preach, and the number of Christians grew steadily to several hundred. He started new churches in Yamaguchi, Hirado, and Bungo.

After being in Japan for about twenty-seven months, Xavier concluded that because Japanese held the Chinese in such high esteem, Christianity must enter Japan from China. He assumed that Japan would imitate China and become Christian.

Therefore, the "saint in a hurry" left Japan in 1551. He went back to Goa and in the same year sailed with a few companions for China. He wanted to evangelize China, but worn out by his labors, he fell ill and died on December 3, 1552 off the coast of China on the island of Shang-ch'uan (Saint John Island).[51] His body is buried in Goa, and the right arm with which he baptized thousands of people is kept in Rome.[52]

In the next part of this essay, I will present five principles that can be learned from the life and ministry of Francis Xavier. As we will see, the first three principles are helpful for a cross-cultural entrepreneurship. The latter two are the result of critical reflections of Francis Xavier's missionary endeavor.

Five Principles from Francis Xavier's Life

This part of the essay analyzes Xavier's life and generates five principles that are relevant for the mission of the church in the twenty-first century. It argues that these principles should be applied in outreach to people in a globalized society.

Principle 1: Be Flexible and Willing to Adjust

As presented earlier, Xavier heard rumors that two kings in southern Celebes had been baptized and asked for missionaries to instruct their peoples. Xavier sailed to Malacca, where he stayed until December 1545. He fought hard against the immorality of the Portuguese and succeeded in a kind of reformation of the city, while trying hard to learn a bit of Malay. Francis's example of a simple, holy, and hardworking life helped him to reach out to the people, even non-Christians. Following his vows as founding member of the Society of Jesus, the example of his lifestyle was important in this context for the people to understand the seriousness of his mission. In the early period of his apostolic mission, he could always refer to his apostolic authority, as he was sent by the pope and the king of Portugal. Therefore, he could criticize the people for their scandalous behavior. Moreover, in India and Malacca, Francis displayed a methodology by which he started with the poor.

When Francis arrived in Japan, however, he realized he had to change his missionary methods. Because the Japanese were afraid of losing their unity, it was important for Francis to start by evangelizing the rulers and not the poor. In the winter of 1550, therefore, he went to Kyoto to meet the emperor and obtain permission to preach in the whole country, but he was not able to obtain an audience or preach to the imperial court. Being a Roman *nuncio* and an official ambassador of the Portuguese king was of no value in Japan unless he represented his status in the ways the Japanese might understand. Apostolic poverty and authority that helped in other places did not help here. He saw for spiritual leaders to be accepted, they had to dress and behave accordingly. So he started to dress in silk and bring gifts in order to win the *daimyo*.[53] Francis was able to contextualize his message without compromising it. He was aware that he himself as messenger is the message for the people. Thus, he became an example for the Jesuit missionaries who followed.[54] Eventually, this helped to develop the Society's principle that "a Jesuit be open and responsive to the situation to which he was called."[55]

To be relevant to the people, the church needs to behave, speak, and live in ways that are attractive to people the church wants to reach. What works in one place might fail in another. This is not only a question of style, such as the clothes people wear or the music we use in our church services. It is also a question of theology. Steven Bevans argues that there is only theology in contexts, and thus contextual theology is imperative for the church.[56] Every local church is concerned with different issues. While in the context of India, poverty and the marginalization of the untouchables was a problem; in the Malaccas it was important for Francis to confront the scandalous behavior of the Portuguese traders; in Japan, it was necessary for him to give answers in discussions with Buddhist clergy.[57] Every situation demanded a different theological adjustment.

Thus, Francis became an illustration for the church how to follow Christ in her mission. Christ himself became incarnate in this world at a particular time and place, first-century Jewish society (John 1:14). Jesus of Nazareth delivered relevant answers for first-century Jewish questions. In the same way, Francis attempted to deliver answers to sixteenth-century Asian issues. The twenty-first-century church is called to do so as well. Therefore, the global church needs appropriate local expressions and theologies. For instance, the church in Europe must deliver answers to a fragmented society with its overwhelming materialism. On the other hand, Asian and African churches are confronted with questions concerning the well-being of their ancestors.

The church will do so because she reflects the love of God to the people.

Principle 2: Respect and Love the People

In the life and ministry of Francis Xavier one can observe a development. In the first period of his work, he still followed a *tabula rasa* approach. Although he accepted the people's language and wanted them to hear the gospel in their vernacular, he insisted on translations of Latin hymns and prayers. In practice, this meant that people who wanted to become Christians had to adopt European culture along with the Christian faith.[58] Moreover, as shown, in India, he did not expect the Indian church to survive without European support. This, however, changed after his arrival in Japan.

In his letters to Ignatius, Francis spoke admiringly of the Japanese people, praising their sense of honor and civility:

> First of all, the people with whom we have thus far conversed are the best that have as yet been discovered; and it seems to me that no other pagan race will be found that will surpass the Japanese. They have, as a race, very fine manners; and they are on the whole good and not malicious. They have a marvelous sense of honor and esteem it more than anything else. As a race they are generally poor, but the poverty that is found among the nobles and those who are not is not deemed to be a matter of reproach."[59]

The Jesuits and Franciscans who followed Xavier in Japan clashed over the implications of his approach,[60] but Matteo Ricci (1552–1610) in China and Roberto de Nobili (1557–1656) in India, followed the lead of Xavier's new methods, and the concept of accommodation became a new understanding and approach to non-European religions. The total rejection of non-European culture was replaced by a search for parallels in concept and form, and a new way of comprehending world culture was introduced. The implications and interpretations of this line of thought are still debated, but for our purposes it can be concluded that Xavier's shift in models of comparison unintentionally contributed to the birth of a new theory of understanding. The American scholar of religion Herb Skoglund discusses how Xavier's opinion changed from a "not-like-us" to a "like-us" model.[61] Coming from Portugal as an ambassador of the king and the pope, Francis had had a different attitude in India and in the Malaccian islands than he had later in Japan, where he could only depend on the hospitality of the Japanese.[62] Enjoying this hospitality helped him to come to a different attitude toward the Japanese.

The American anthropologist R. Dan Shaw urges the church to be able not only to preach to the people but to respect them so much as to be willing to learn from them.[63] For example, missionaries should ask themselves what they might learn from the people in Malawi, Africa. Church workers in an inner-city mission should not look down on the homeless but respect them and treat them as equals. It must be an intercultural principle of the church in the globalized world of the twenty-first century to invite people to the church's fellowship. They neither must become American nor European-style Christians. They are welcomed to follow Christ in their cultures.

This is significant for the people who are willing to follow the church's call to enter the Christian faith, and it is also crucial in the encounter with other religious traditions. We will see this in the next principle.

Principle 3: Think Beyond Christian Parameters

In Japan, Xavier had many discussions with the Buddhist clergy. He noticed that he could not argue with the apostolic authority and power of the church but needed what the missiologists from the Bevans and Schroeder call "prophetic dialogue" that is modeled on Christ's way of humility and self-emptying (Phil 2:5–11), but at the same time "a bold proclamation of God's already and not-yet reign."[64] This is furthermore reflected in Xavier's attitude toward the religious Japanese traditions.

Francis Xavier recognized that ancestor worship was the root of the faith and strength of blood ties in Japan. He learned that the most important concern of the Japanese people was the salvation of the dead, especially blood relations, from hell. How to deal with the salvation of the dead was therefore the most important problem that missionaries faced. Although Xavier could not reconcile it with Christianity, identifying it made him successful.

In contrast to Xavier, the Australian professor for Japanese studies Mark Mullins argues that this was the Western Protestant missionaries' mistake in Japanese culture. "The missionary view was that various indigenous traditions would need to be displaced[65] to make room for the Gospel and authentic Christian faith. The gospel preached by most missionaries included the teaching that there is no hope for those who die without faith in Christ."[66] This reflects a colonial mindset that expects the people to leave their being Japanese at the entrance when they want to enter the church.

Concerning ancestor veneration, Xavier was willing to engage with this crucial topic of Japanese culture and religious sensation with an open mind without a fear of syncretism. This paper does not want to answer the question whether non-Christian religions have salvific meaning but argues that mission must include an openness to real dialogue to learn from their understanding and wisdom that the Holy Spirit has placed in them. As the Vatican II decree *Ad Gentes* puts it,

> *Even as Christ Himself searched the hearts of men, and led them to divine light, so also His disciples, profoundly penetrated by the Spirit of Christ, should show the people among whom they live, and should converse with them, that they themselves may learn by sincere and patient dialogue what treasures a generous God has distributed among the nations of the earth. But at the same time, let them try to furbish these treasures, set them free, and bring them under the dominion of God their Savior.[67]*

The Christian church must do so with scripture in her hand. True dialogue does not mean to take over all that others say; true dialogue means to have a firm stand in one's own position, but to listen and attempt to understand. True dialogue does not turn down the adherents of other faiths but grants them the freedom to live out their faith. It follows Christ on the road to Emmaus. He dialogued with the disciples and gave them understanding of his suffering. He did not force them to take him into their house, but "he walked ahead as if he were going on." However, when they urged the resurrected Jesus to come in, they noticed that they did not host him, but they were guests at his table (Luke 24:13–35). Therefore, Christian missionary dialogue means to invite the adherents of other faiths to the table of Christ, but always respecting their faith and freedom to reject this invitation. In this kind of dialogue, Christians will not urge the other; like Jesus, they will walk ahead as if "[they] were going on" (Luke 24:28).

The following two principles are lessons that could be learned from Xavier's flaws. The church is always well advised to learn from the past. We do not honor the saints of the past by neglecting their mistakes, but we honor them by learning from their whole lives, in order to improve the ministry of the church.

Principle 4: The Church Must Be Fluent in the Language

While in India, Francis stressed the importance of translation. In Japan, he wished to learn the language because he observed how Anjirô preached to his family and converted them.[68] Unfortunately, Francis was unable to speak Japanese well. He simply was not there long enough to master the language at a time when there were no textbooks or language schools. He relied on Juan Fernandez, who was proficient in the language, and two talented Japanese: Bernard, who accompanied him on his travels throughout Japan, and a blind minstrel, Brother Laurence. Moreover, Anjirô translated certain Christian messages into Japanese, so that the people could read them without interacting with the missionaries. Anjirô, however, was uneducated. Because he did not have deep knowledge of his own culture and religious traditions, it was only to be expected that his translations were imperfect. Aoyama alleges that choosing Anjirô as translator was a mistake because he did not have the education of a member of the warrior class.[69]

The problem became evident when Anjirô chose to translate the Latin *deus* into the Buddhist term *dainichi*, the Shingon Buddhist sun god,[70] which evokes a completely different image of God. The church in Japan struggles with this issue to this day.

Francis always had an ambivalent relationship to languages. He grew up speaking Basque while surrounded by Spanish speakers. In Paris, he focused on Latin. He learned Greek and Hebrew, which at that time was mostly done by Protestants because they focused on translating the Bible from the original languages. In Goa, he started by translating Christian prayers, hymns, sermons, and other catechetical material into the vernacular. In all places he ministered, he attempted to learn the language, but he never attained proficiency.

By translating into the vernacular and working to learn the local languages, Francis showed respect to the local people. This was also a theological decision. The African historian of mission, Lamin Sanneh, says, "Mission as translation makes the bold, fundamental assertion that the recipient culture is the authentic destination of God's salvific promise and, as a consequence, has an honored place under the kindness of God, with the attendant safeguards against cultural absolutism."[71] In other words, by translating into Tamil, Xavier showed that he regarded the Indian Christians as equally deserving of God's salvation as the Europeans were.

The Protestant Reformation, with its motto taken from Humanists' *ad fontes*, "to the sources," was about translation. Martin Luther's translation of the Bible into German fueled the Reformation and spiritual renewal in Germany. Now every person could read or listen to the scripture and understand it. The Roman Catholic Church has developed a greater awareness of the vernacular after Vatican II. Especially *Sacrosanctum Concilium* recommends the use of the vernacular in liturgy: "In Masses which are celebrated with the people, a suitable place may be allotted to their mother tongue. This is to apply in the first place to the readings and 'the common prayer,' but also, as local conditions may warrant, to those parts which pertain to the people."[72]

It seems that Francis himself would support this because he wanted translations into Tamil. Unfortunately, he was unable to learn Japanese because he was not in Japan long enough to gain proficiency, a topic to be discussed in the next principle.

In her intercultural entrepreneurship of global mission, the church is asked to wrestle with the vernacular to deepen the roots of Christianity in a specific cultural group. It thus builds on a crucial tradition. The first Greek translation of the Old Testament was done by Hellenistic Jews between 250 and 100 BC. The Septuagint that can be found even in New Testament quotations are evidence that there is no such thing as a holy language. The Jewish Septuagint translators even dared to translate the Tetragram (יהוה) that refers to God's name (Exod 20:2–3) and Jews normally read as *adonai*, "my lord," or *ha shem*, "the name," into the Greek *kyrios* that is commonly rendered in English as LORD. In this tradition the church is asked to strive for theological expressions that foster an image of God that is relevant to the people and simultaneously close to the biblical revelation of the triune God. Anjirô chose *dainichi*, which commonly referred to a Buddhist deity. Whether or not this was a good choice is for us to decide. Furthermore, fluency in a language means using relevant means of communicating the gospel to the world. A twenty-first-century church needs fluency in the language of the internet, just as Paul could communicate with the Greek philosophers in the marketplace of Athens as well as with the Jews in the synagogue (Acts 17:17–18). He was fluent in their ways of communication.

Fluency in a language is not attained by simply learning the grammar and the vocabulary. It means to be aware of what the people are concerned about. The church is always placed in a specific culture, and it must know the culture to speak to the culture. Like the Old Testament prophet

Daniel, who was deported to Babylon, the church will always be foreign, but like Daniel, it will only be relevant and have an impact if she is willing to learn like Daniel the "literature and language of the Chaldeans [Babylonians]" (Dan 1:4).

Daniel studied the Babylonian culture for three years and stayed in Babylon until the end of his life. He was a lifelong learner of what it means to belong to the people of God in a foreign land. Francis Xavier was in Japan only for about twenty-seven months. To know the culture and influence takes time.

Principle 5: Intercultural Entrepreneurship Needs Time

Xavier seems to have been in a great hurry in the last ten years of his life. He did not stay in one place for long but rushed on to the next. One might argue Paul did the same in his mission journeys recorded in Acts. However, unlike Francis, who moved among a variety of cultures, Paul did not leave the Roman-Hellenistic culture.

After being in Japan for little more than two years, Francis Xavier wanted to reach the Japanese via the Chinese and left for Goa to sail to China. He noticed that the Japanese regard the Chinese culture as superior, and he concluded that once the Chinese would be converted, the Japanese would follow, so he went to China where he passed away on December 3, 1552.

Thus, he was in Japan for too short a time. His successors continued his work and organized and consolidated, but not all did it the way Xavier would have. The Italian Alessandro Valignano, Xavier's direct successor in Japan, followed his ways. He developed a "gentle way" of encounter with adherents of other religions and was successful. Valignano ordained Japanese priests and started seminaries to educate Japanese Christians. He ordered that priests should be dressed in silk clothes like Zen Buddhist monks to accommodate themselves to Japanese culture.

Later, however, the clash between the Jesuits and the Franciscans led to internal divisions.[73] They debated about the priests' clothing, whether they should wear silk or dress poorly, as the Franciscans did in Europe.[74] In the long run, this led to the alienation of Christianity in Japan and to persecution of Christians because the government regarded Christians as a danger to the country's unity. Eventually the Japanese government banished all missionaries and closed off the country.

In comparison to Francis Xavier, the Jesuit missionary to China Matteo Ricci (1552–1610), lived in China for twenty-eight years from 1582 until 1610. Moreover, the Baptist missionary William Carey (1761–1834) stayed in India for forty-one years, from 1793 until his death in 1834. The founder of the China Inland Mission, James Hudson Taylor (1832–1905), spent thirty-nine years in China from 1866 until 1905. The list could be continued. The argument is that the longer missionaries stay in a culture, the greater the chance that their mission will take deep roots. This is a significant principle for the individual missionary as well as for the whole church.

In the twenty-first century, the church is tempted to strive for quick results. Western culture is influenced by materialistic business ways of thinking that search for quick success. This attitude does not stop at the doors of the church, but, following its master Jesus of Nazareth, the church must learn to take time. Just as the eternal Word of God set up his tent among humans (John 1:14),[75] the church is called to live among the people. Jesus waited thirty years before he started his public ministry. He was willing to take time to learn the culture and the language. He identified with the people completely.

Conclusion

Francis Xavier was an intercultural *avant-gardist*. He had to undergo a change in his mindset from the *tabula rasa* method that had worked in Portuguese territories to a methodology that respected the culture and religious tradition of the places he worked. Due to this cultural sensitivity, he opened new ways of thinking for the global church to reach out to people groups who were foreign to the gospel. Later missionaries like Valignano, Ricci, and the Protestant missionaries used his experiences to develop concepts such as accommodation, inculturation, and contextualization.

We live in a globalized world in which meeting your next-door neighbor may be an intercultural experience. Due to the movement of refugees in Europe, even in smaller countryside cities, at least twenty-five cultural groups can be living in one city. The church does well to listen and examine the ways and experiences of this saint in the past. Many of his principles are still significant for a Christian entrepreneurship in the twenty-first century, an entrepreneurship that takes seriously cultural differences as well as rejects a Euro- or America-centric attitude, so that the mission of the church will be more effective *Ad maiorem Dei Gloria*, "for the greater glory of God."

Notes

1. Klaus Schatz, "Franz Xaver," in *Lexikon für Theologie und Kirche*, ed. Walter Kasper, et al. (Freiburg im Breisgau: Herder, 2009), 56.

2. P. A. De Rover and Julius Roessle, *Gottes Spur ist Überall: Eine Geschichte der Weltmission in Einzelbildern* (Konstanz: Christliche Verlagsanstalt, 1960), 113. This is not an academic book, rather it is a hagiography of influential persons in the history of the mission of the church.

3. Stephen B. Bevans and Roger Schroeder, *Constants in Context: A Theology of Mission for Today*, American Society of Missiology Series 30 (Maryknoll, NY: Orbis Books, 2004), 366. He was canonized in 1622. Jesus Lopez-Gay, "Francis Xavier," in *Biographical Dictionary of Christian Missions*, ed. Gerald H. Anderson (Grand Rapids, MI: William B. Eerdmans, 1998), 751.

4. Georg Schurhammer, *Francis Xavier* (Rome: Jesuit Historical Institute, 1973).

5. The term *church* refers here to the one church consisting of all Christians baptized in the name of the trinitarian God (Eph 4). This one church, however, contains four "major families which involves the Roman Catholic church, the Orthodox churches, the churches of the Reformation and the Pentecostal churches." Scott W. Sunquist, *Understanding Christian Mission: Participation in Suffering and Glory* (Grand Rapids, MI: Baker, 2013), 43. Furthermore, this one church becomes visible through several expressions of local churches.

6. Schurhammer, *Francis Xavier*, 19.

7. Herb Skoglund, "St. Francis Xavier's Encounter with Japan," *Missiology: An International Review* 3, no. 4 (1975): 464.

8. Friedrich Wilhelm Bautz, "Franz Xaver," in *Biographisch-Bibliographisches Kirchenlexikon* (Hamm: Verlag Traugott Bautz, 1975), 109.

9. Schurhammer, *Francis Xavier*, 46.

10. De Rover und Roessle, *Gottes Spur ist Überall*, 111.

11. Schurhammer is not sure about this statement (Schurhammer, *Francis Xavier*, 119). On the other hand, the Protestant historians, De Rover and Roessle allege that Francis loved to hear Calvin (De Rover and Roessle, *Gottes Spur ist Überall*, 111). It can be assumed that Francis was in touch with Calvin, but his roots in the tradition of the Roman church in which he was raised were much stronger than the fascination of a new teaching. Thus, it is unlikely that he was tempted to become a Protestant.

12. Schurhammer, *Francis Xavier*, 119.

13. Dale T. Irvin and Scott W. Sunquist, *History of the World Christian Movement*, vol. 2 of *Modern Christianity from 1454–1800* (Maryknoll, NY: Orbis Books, 2012), 115.

14. Michael Hanst, "Ignatius von Loyola," in *Biographisch-Bibliographisches Kirchenlexikon*, ed. Friedrich Wilhelm Bautz and Traugott Bautz (Hamm: Verlag Traugott Bautz, 1990), 1528.

15. Hanst, "Ignatius von Loyola," 1259.

16. The Frenchman Peter Favre was also a founding member of the Society of Jesus. James Martin, "Blessed Peter Favre and Friendship," *America*, August 2, 2012, https://www.americamagazine.org/content/all-things/blessed-peter-favre-and-friendship. Martin shows how significant friendship was for the founders of the Jesuits throughout their lives. This is a crucial factor for the well-being of priest and ministers. Having close and trusted friends helps to get through the trouble of everyday parish life as well as the challenges of intercultural mission.

17. Schurhammer, *Francis Xavier*, 119.

18. Schurhammer, *Francis Xavier*, 154.

19. Martin, "Blessed Peter Favre and Friendship."

20. Lopez-Gay, "Francis Xavier," 751.

21. Schurhammer, *Francis Xavier*, 223.

22. Schurhammer, *Francis Xavier*, 214. For a description of the *Spiritual Exercises*, see Irvin and Sunquist, *History of the World Christian Movement*, 115–17. The *Spiritual Exercises* are merely meant to be spiritual not physical.

23. Henry Venn, *The Missionary Life and Labours of Francis Xavier Taken from His Own Correspondence: With a Sketch of the General Results of Roman Catholic Missions among the Heathen* (Cambridge: Cambridge University Press, 2010), 7, http://dx.doi.org/10.1017/CBO9780511697838.

24. Irvin and Sunquist, *History of World Christian Movement*, 119; Hanst, "Ignatius von Loyola," 1259.

25. Irvin and Sunquist, *History of World Christian Movement*, 62.

26. Bautz, "Franz Xaver," 109.

27. Irvin and Sunquist, *History of World Christian Movement*, 118; Hanst, "Ignatius von Loyola," 1259.

28. Irvin and Sunquist, *History of World Christian Movement*, 62.

29. De Rover und Roessle, *Gottes Spur ist Überall*, 112.

30. Irvin and Sunquist, *History of World Christian Movement*, 62.

31. De Rover und Roessle, *Gottes Spur ist Überall*, 112.

32. De Rover und Roessle, *Gottes Spur ist Überall*, 112.

33. Teotonio R. De Souza and Charles J. Borges, *Jesuits in India: In Historical Perspective* (Macao: Instituto Cultural de Macau, 1992), 77.

34. Irvin and Sunquist, *History of World Christian Movement*, 62.

35. Bevans and Schroeder, *Constants in Context*, 185.

36. Bevans and Schroeder, *Constants in Context*, 184.

37. See Acts 13:5, 14; 14:1; 17:1, 30.

38. The name *Anjirô* seems unusual for a Japanese. Later he was named Paul of the Holy Faith. A detailed description of his life can be found in Gen Paul Aoyama, *Die Missionstätigkeit des heiligen Franz Xaver in Japan aus japanischer Sicht*, Studia Instituti Missiologici Societatis Verbi Divini 10 (Sankt Augustin: Steyler Verlag, 1967), 24.

39. Bevans and Schroeder, *Constants in Context*, 184.

40. Irvin and Sunquist, *History of World Christian Movement*, 64.

41. Aoyama, *Missionstaetigkeit des Hl. Franz Xaver*, 26.

42. P. Cosme de Torres and Br. Juan Fernandez; Aoyama, *Missionstaetigkeit des Hl. Franz Xaver*, 42.

43. For a detailed discussion of Anjirô's linguistic mistakes, see Aoyama, *Missionstaetigkeit des Hl. Franz Xaver*.

44. Irvin and Sunquist allege that after Anjirô suffered persecution in Japan, he eventually fled Japan for good and abandoned Christianity, dying as a pirate in China. Irvin and Sundquist, *History of World Christian Movement*, 64–65.

45. Lopez-Gay, "Francis Xavier," 751.

46. Aoyama, *Missionstaetigkeit des Hl. Franz Xaver*, 46.

47. Bevans and Schroeder, *Constants in Contexts*, 185.

48. Schatz, "Franz Xaver," 56.

49. Claudia von Collani, "Xavier, Franz," in *Biographisch-Bibliographisches Kirchenlexikon*, ed. Friedrich Wilhelm Bautz and Traugott Bautz (Hamm: Bautz, 1998), 270.

50. Laurence was baptized by Francis Xavier in 1551. After Xavier left Japan, he became a significant evangelist in Japan because of his proficiency in music. Shuma Iwai, "An Analysis of Francis Xavier's Letters from Kagoshima, Japan (1549): His Approaches and Views of Ministry," *Asia Journal of Theology* 21, no. 1 (2007): 13.

51. Lopez-Gay, "Francis Xavier," 751.

52. Schatz, "Franz Xaver," 56.

53. Aoyama writes about meetings between Francis and the lords, in which he gives them pictures of Mary and the lords' enthusiastic reactions. Aoyama, *Missionstaetigkeit des Hl. Franz Xaver*.

54. Alessandro Valignano (1539–1606) built his methodological concept of accommodation, what he called *il modo soave*, "the sweet or gentle way," on Xavier's methods. This helped the Jesuits to succeed in China, especially the Italian Matteo Ricci. Von Collani, "Xavier," 270.

55. Bevans and Schroeder, *Constants in Context*, 186.

56. Stephen B. Bevans, *Models of Contextual Theology*, rev. and exp. ed., Faith and Cultures Series (Maryknoll, NY: Orbis Books, 2002), 1–3.

57. Schatz, "Franz Xaver," 55.

58. Bevans and Schroeder, *Constants in Context*, 185.

59. Found in Iwai, "Analysis of Francis Xavier's Letters," 8.

60. Irvin and Sunquist, *History of World Christian Movement*, 162.

61. Skoglund, "Xavier's Encounter with Japan," 451.

62. Here he followed what Jesus demanded from his disciples, "When you enter a town, eat what is set before you" (Luke 10:8, NIV; see Matt 10:5–15, Mark 6:7–13).

63. R. Daniel Shaw, "Beyond Contextualization: Toward a Twenty-First-Century Model for Enabling Mission," *International Bulletin of Missionary Research* 34, no. 4 (2010): 211.

64. Bevans and Schroeder, *Constants in Context*, 284–85.

65. *Tabula rasa*: It seems the Protestants had the same tendencies, only three hundred years later.

66. Mark Mullins, *Christianity Made in Japan: A Study of Indigenous Movements*, Nanzan Library of Asian Religion and Culture (Honolulu: University of Hawai'i Press, 1998), 135.

67. Vatican Council II, *Ad Gentes* (On the Mission Activity of the Church), no. 11, http://www.vatican.va/archive/hist_councils/ii_vatican_council/documents/vat-ii_decree_19651207_ad-gentes_en.html. Cf. Pater Pervia's letter to the SVD missionaries in which he suggests changing the concept from *ad gentes* to *inter gentes*, in which mission becomes an enterprise of all Christians who live among secular people or other religions. Antonio Pervia, "Ein Wort von Pater General-Missio Inter Gentes," May 3, 2010, accessed August 16, 2018, https://iwm.sankt-georgen.de/von-ad-gentes-zu-inter-gentes/.

68. Iwai, "Analysis of Francis Xavier's Letters," 10.

69. Aoyama, "Missionstaetigkeit des Hl. Franz Xaver," 31.

70. Iwai, "Analysis of Francis Xavier's Letters," 11.

71. Lamin O. Sanneh, *Translating the Message: The Missionary Impact on Culture*, 2nd ed. rev. and exp., American Society of Missiology Series 42 (Maryknoll, NY: Orbis Books, 2009), 31.

72. Vatican Council II, *Sacrosanctum Concilium* (Constitution on the Sacred Liturgy), no. 54. http://www.vatican.va/archive/hist_councils/ii_vatican_council/documents/vat-ii_const_1963 1204_sacrosanctum-concilium_en.html.

73. Irvin and Sunquist, *History of World Christian Movement*, 161–62.

74. Josef Franz Schütte, *Valignanos Missionsgrundsätze für Japan* (Rome: Storia e Letteratura, 1951), 271.

75. Pervia, "Ein Wort."

9

Ecclesiastical Crowdfunding

An Innovative Form of Church Financing

Christoph Biermeier

Introduction and the Managerial Challenge

Matthew 18:20 says, "For where two or three are gathered in my name, I am there among them." Transferring this into the context of managerial situations in the church, we can also state that here cooperation is part of Christian identity and Christian social teaching. We find this spirit in ecclesiastical crowdfunding—a recently emerged form of church financing—as it realizes the principle of subsidiarity in a form of self-responsibility. *Crowdfunding* is defined as "the practice of obtaining needed funding (as for a new business) by soliciting contributions from a large number of people especially from the internet."[1] In practice, there are many small parish projects that cannot be realized due to a lack of funding. Examples of such projects are the refurbishment of a church flag or a new swing set for the parish kindergarten. Additionally, organizing for the necessary financial means can be time-consuming. This is where crowdfunding can help as it only requires an internet platform or a mobile phone app to organize microfinancing for the specific project. Ideally, the platform is free of charge for both sides, that is, the project coordinator(s) and the donors/investors. Donors in turn, can be acknowledged by a simple thank-you, small gift, or plaque once the project is complete.[2]

The Functioning of Ecclesiastical Crowdfunding
The Idea behind Crowdfunding

The term *crowdfunding* consists of two words: *crowd* and *funding*. This means that many people give funding for a specific purpose, and this crowd meets virtually on a digital platform. A key feature of crowdfunding is that the advertisement of the project happens on electronic platforms such as the crowdfunding website itself or social media such as Facebook, Twitter, or Instagram. Additionally, it is important to note that the collected funds are earmarked, which means they can only be used for a specific purpose, the purpose set by the project's initiator.

An example where both forms, successful funding and media attention, worked out very well is when U.S. rock legend Jon Bon Jovi donated to the project "My Dad Has a Trauma," initiated by the German Catholic Family Foundation for soldiers. He was able to donate to the campaign from New York even though the project was in Germany. This was made possible by Lieutenant W. of the Tactical Air Force Squadron 51 and his personal contact with the singer's family. Thus, he had asked if support for the project in the form of a guitar from the band for an auction would be possible. Instead, Jon Bon Jovi donated directly to the crowdfunding project via the internet.[3]

Donation Portals and Examples of Crowdfunding

Crowdfunding is not equivalent to the use of donation portals. In the case of donation portals, supporters donate to an organization or a specific project without a time frame. In contrast, crowdfunding is conducted within a given period. Also, where in the case of donation portals supporters or donors receive nothing in return, this can be different in crowdfunding. In either case, supporters receive a thank-you in some form. A Catholic example of a donation portal is www.missio.org, which also offers its services in an app. Missio.org was initiated by the Pontifical Mission Societies in the United States. Regarding this, Oblate Father Andrew Small stated in an interview with Catholic News Service that the internet "is the great connector, so we looked at how we could put this amazing technology that connects people instantaneously," together with the great millennia-old human network of the church.[4]

Beyond that, donation portals usually aim to reach a certain donation amount and are terminated once the amount has been reached. In contrast, crowdfunding also aims to reach for a certain amount but within a time frame with an "all or nothing" stipulation, which means that if the amount is not reached within the time frame, then all donations will be refunded and the project will not be realized. Due to this, it is of key importance that the project is well planned and accompanied by a well-designed campaign.

Typically, crowdfunding projects are publicized for ninety days and entail project amounts of about $500 to $10,000. In practice, there are four forms of crowdfunding:

    (a)   lending-based crowdfunding (crowdlending),

    (b)   equity-based crowdfunding (crowdinvesting),

    (c)   reward-based crowdfunding, and

    (d)   donation-based crowdfunding.

Where in (a) crowdlending a supporter only gives a loan to the beneficiary expecting a return with interest, (b) crowdinvesting indicates participation with equity and allows the supporter to receive a return on future earnings of the project. In contrast to this, in (c) reward-based crowdfunding, the supporter donates within a specific period for a specific project and receives a service in return, for example, a small gift. The fourth manifestation (d) donation-based crowdfunding is like (c), but in this case supporters donate within a specific period for a specific project and receive nothing in return. Table 1 below gives an overview of the four forms.

Type of Crowdfunding	Fixed Duration	Fixed Amount	Refund if Campaign Unsuccessful
Crowdlending	Yes	Yes	No
Crowdinvesting	Yes	Yes	No
Crowdfunding			
—with gift	Yes	Yes	Yes
—without gift	Yes	Yes	Yes

Table 1: Crowdfunding overview (compiled by author).

In the German example for such a platform—www.wo2oder3.de (offered by PAX Bank, a Catholic Church bank in Germany)—all transaction costs are covered by the bank as support for the project.

Also, PAX Bank supports every project that is accepted with an additional donation—so-called *co-funding*. Thus, each individual donation of at least $11 is co-funded by another $5.50 by PAX Bank.

The Different Stages of a Campaign

A typical crowdfunding project with PAX Bank consists of three major phases. First, there is the project *setup phase*: the project opens an account with PAX Bank and the initiator must be "tax-privileged" (i.e., a recognized charitable organization). Next is the *backer phase* of about fourteen days. Here it is necessary to discern how many people are likely to back the project—usually between twenty and one hundred prospective supporters are required. A minimum of twenty indicates financing of $550–$1,100, and one hundred supporters indicates up to $11,200. This can happen using an existing Facebook account or registration on the platform. Here, data protection is of major importance and the donors' information is not forwarded to the bank or project initiator. After that is the actual *financing phase* of about ninety days, during which it is possible to donate either by registering or as an unregistered guest. It is also possible to make an anonymous donation. Figure 1 below summarizes the distinct phases of a campaign.

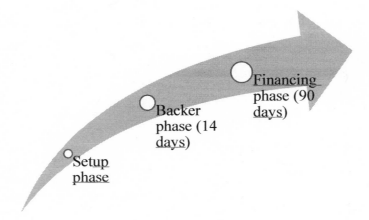

Figure 1: The distinct phases of crowdfunding (diagram based on illustration by PAX Bank).

PAX Bank supports reward-based crowdfunding, where the donor receives either a receipt or a thank-you in the form of a small service or gift sent by the project initiator, such as a thank-you letter, a button, or invitation to an event. There must be consideration of value: material acknowledgments such as gifts can affect the donor's taxes and must be included on tax returns. In practice, this often is not an issue because the acknowledgment is often simply a note and nothing of tangible value.

Unsuccessful and Over-Subscribed Campaigns

Occasionally, projects do not raise the target amount, in which case donations are refunded to the original donors. This is due to the all-or-nothing principle of crowdfunding and secures the donors as it ensures that the amount necessary to realize the project is raised. In case of PAX Bank, co-funding remains with the project initiator as a donation, regardless of the campaign's success or failure.

In contrast, there are also highly successful campaigns where donations exceed the target amount. In this case, the additional amount must be reviewed. Crowdfunding donations are earmarked, and the excess cannot be used for another purpose without the consent of the donor. Portals often include a section in the project description that states what will happen to excess funds if the project is over-subscribed.

Communication, the Key for Successful Campaigns

A successful crowdfunding campaign must have particularly effective communication, whether in the form of emails or blog entries. In practice, a blog gives the most contact with donors.

It is essential that the project have a dedicated contact person and a realistic goal. If a parish collects for a new swing set for its kindergarten, the amount would probably be more modest, for example, between $550 and $2,800. Additionally, it is important that the project initiators are not averse to using social media. It is vital that the project initiators have a presence on social media and advertise the project through various channels. Also, it is important that the project initiators do not promote more than one project at once. This can lead to mistrust and a situation where the different projects are no longer manageable. Ultimately, it is important to prepare the project well and to have an initial backer base.

Conclusion

Church financing in the twenty-first century is different than it was a hundred years ago. The environment has changed significantly in the Western world; that is, the obvious conditions are no longer industrialization and urbanization but secularization and digitalization. Those making decisions in the church must adapt to the new environment. Here, crowdfunding can be an additional pillar of any church financing system. Not only does it allow the use of social media for the sake of the mission, but also has a community character. Crowdfunding will probably not solve all the financial problems of the global church, but it can form a new relationship between donors and the church, and it especially gives acknowledgment to those who actually initiate and realize charitable projects. This attention for the people of the project itself appears to be a most valuable aspect of crowdfunding.

Notes

1. *Merriam-Webster,* s.v "crowdfunding," n.d. Retrieved from https://www.merriam-webster .com/dictionary/crowdfunding.

2. PAX Bank, s.v. "Crowdfunding—der Weg zum Ziel" ("Crowdfunding—The Way to Your Goal"), 2019, accessed October 16, 2020, https://www.pax-bank.de/content/dam/f0395-0/ interneinhalte/pdf/flyer/2019_wo2oder3_Flyer.pdf.

3. wo2oder3.de, "Projektblog—Mein Papa hat Trauma. Katholische Familienstiftung für Soldaten" ("Project Blog—My Dad Has a Trauma. Catholic Family Foundation for Soldiers"), n.d., accessed October 16, 2020, https://www.wo2oder3.de/meinpapahattrauma/blog/.

4. Carol Glatz, "Bots, Apps, Trips: U.S. Mission Societies Connect People in Many Ways," *The Catholic Telegraph*, May 11, 2017, https://www.thecatholictelegraph.com/bots-apps-trips-u-s -mission-societies-connect-people-in-many-ways/41896.

10

The "Two-Hat" Theory of Management

A Pastor's Role in Performance Management

Declan Cahill

Introduction

In 2010, Charles Zech published an edited collection of contributing authors in which the focus was performance management (PM).[1] My contribution to our current Festival is also PM and I was invited to this gathering to speak to you about my current research on PM, in the context of church management in Ireland. The approach I am taking in this paper and in my presentation to you is to start by looking back to 2010. What were the themes and issues addressed in that book? What did we learn about PM and the church then? I will then reflect on how those themes resonate today. Are they still relevant? Have the issues been addressed, do they still exist, are there new concerns? My reflection will be grounded in my own study of PM over the past six years, and my historical and current experience of working with priests/brothers in their spiritual and managerial domains. In the latter part of this paper, I will propose that our focus on PM is missing a crucial step. Drawing on my current research with priests/brothers who inhabit both spiritual and managerial roles in the conduct of their pastoral duties, I will suggest that a real understanding of PM in faith-based settings is missing a step, to be underpinned by an appreciation and understanding of what the priests/brothers have to say about what it means to them to be a manager. To be able to really develop a PM context requires that first we understand what it means for a priest/brother to be a manager.

This paper is organized as follows: I start by introducing the context for PM in the church. Why is it important? This contextual introduction will draw both on my personal experience in difficult PM contexts, and on what the literature says is important about PM for religious contexts.

Next, I will turn to the detailed work discussed in the 2010 book. What did the contributors have to stay about PM? What did they see as the issues that PM could address, and how did they see PM addressing these?

As I discuss the contributions from 2010, I will comment on them with reference to their relevance in 2018. To what extent have these issues been addressed and dispatched already? Which of them are still relevant? Are there any new themes not addressed in 2010?

I will then invite you to consider the PM frame as presented in the 2010 publication with a critical eye. I will summarize where I think we are now with the PM concept, and how that compares with where we were in 2010. I will argue that there is an important missing step in the process. PM is predicated on the assumption that we know what religious (appendix A) are doing when they manage, and that we know how they think or feel about it. My current research argues that we do not know, and that having an in-depth understanding of the management hat that religious wear is a critical precursor to the development and implementation of an appropriate PM.

I will conclude my discussion by summarizing where we are now. What did we learn in 2010? What is similar and different in 2018? How can a focus on religious' understanding of their management role or what management is underpin a fit-for-purpose approach to PM in 2018? And finally, bringing us back to the purpose of this gathering, I will comment on how my research contributes to this aim of identifying new pastoral ways to proclaim the gospel in a changing world. I look forward very much to contributing to this community of research, exchange, and development of innovative solutions to church management challenges.

The Context for Performance Management in the Church

I start by introducing the context for my study of PM in the church. This contextual introduction draws both on my personal experience in difficult PM contexts, and on what the literature says is important about PM for religious contexts. I completed my masters in management in 2015 with a focus on performance management (PM) and started my PhD with a real determination to "fix" what I saw as persistent managerial problems in religious life. Over the last three years, Dr. Donnelly-Cox in Trinity College has supported me in my inquiry and my continued delving into the PM literature. At the same time, she has pushed me to think critically about what I can and cannot do within the PhD, which is ultimately about "making a contribution" to knowledge rather than solving workplace dilemmas.

Prior to starting PhD research, I spent over thirty-five years in business at every level, including owner, where I had the opportunity to be part of, implement, and use many PM systems. I have seen firsthand the success and failure of PM. Alongside this business life, I have had the opportunity to work with a group of priests, brothers, and laypeople on many community and social projects. While working with the priests, I became very aware that religious wear "two hats." This point was clearly discussed in Zech[2] and validated by many of the book's contributors.[3] The first hat is their "spiritual" role (ontological), who they are, and the second hat is the managerial role (functional) to which they can be assigned, in which they will find themselves managing people and complex organizations.[4] Wearing two hats requires religious to switch back and forth between their pastoral responsibilities/duties (appendix B) and performing their appointed "management roles" (prior, bursar, parish priest, etc.). They operate a medium- to large-sized company, covering everything from strategic planning, HR, director duties, financial management, and project management. The list includes about everything a well-trained team of managers does for a company. So the real origin of my research lay in frustration, as I observed the religious conduct their appointed "management duties" inefficiently and without reference to good business standards. As a good priest friend of mine said, "When religious are appointed to wear hat number 2, competencies are assumed." I became concerned about the implications of "poor management" practice for the work of the religious, their communities, and their constituencies.

Concern about what constitutes "good management" led me down many paths. I started my journey with a focus on PM and a conviction that it would provide a framework within which to conduct doctoral studies. My plan initially was to draw on my extensive business experience and its use of PM within each business discipline and consider its application within a faith-based organization. In reviewing the literature on PM, I found little evidence of extensive application in the domain of faith-based organizations. Despite this, there were many difficulties in applying a PM framework that I discuss below.

Constructing a Definition

I return to the simple definition of PM from *Merriam-Webster*:

Performance **is the execution of an action.**

Management **is the act or art of managing.**

I use these simplified definitions as a foundation for my definition. After much exposure in my business life, my studies, and my work for religious, I now know and understand the negative effect of these words. Proof of the power of words! This negativity stems, I believe, from the control techniques used in the corporate world for many years where the primary goal was not the development of individuals or their well-being, all under the umbrella titled Performance Management. So, to continue to develop a more holistic definition, I turn to the definition from Armstrong and Baron,[5] who give a more holistic view of a PM framework.

Paraphrasing their definition (in italics) in the context of a religious organization that is very much a framework, it can be defined *as a systematic process for improving organizational performance* (we cannot deny that the church needs this) *by developing the performance of individuals and teams* (the word is *develop*, not make or force people). *It is a means of getting better results from (for) the organization, teams, and individuals by* **understanding** *and managing performance* (n.b., making sure you are doing the right thing should not be seen as negative[6]) *within an agreed framework of planned goals, standards, and* **competence** *requirements…processes exist for establishing shared understanding about what is to be achieved, and for managing and developing people in a way that increases the probability that it will be achieved in the short and longer term. Performance management is a strategic and integrated approach to delivering sustained success to organizations by improving the performance of the people who work in them and by developing the capabilities of teams* (e.g., a parish council) *and individual contributors* (could be religious or laypeople—an admirable strategic goal could be to ensure the well-being of all our religious!).[7]

The overall aim of performance management is to establish a high-performance culture in which individuals and teams take responsibility for the continuous improvement and for their own skills and contributions within a framework provided by effective leadership. (Why should this not be the church?) *Its key purpose is to focus people on doing the right things by achieving goal clarity. Specifically, performance management is about aligning individual objectives* (parish priest, bursar, prior) *to organizational objectives* (the order, the church, the archdiocese, Rome) *and ensuring that individuals uphold corporate* (church) *core values. It provides for expectations to be defined and agreed in terms of role responsibilities and accountabilities* (expected to do), *skills* (expected to have), *and behaviors* (expected to be). *The aim is to develop the capacity of people to meet and exceed expectations and to achieve their full potential to the benefit of themselves and the organization* (the church). *Importantly,* **PM is concerned with ensuring that the support and guidance people need to develop and improve are readily available**.[8] I appreciate that the above description of PM is a lofty pursuit, but I do not see any threat to the individual religious or the church in this definition. My next three years of research will seek to clarify this.

Performance Management and the Church: Looking Back to 2010 and Considering the Present

Next, I will turn to the detailed work conducted for the 2010 publication. What did the contributors to the 2010 volume have to stay about PM? What did they see as the issues that PM could address, and how did they see PM addressing these?

As I discuss the contributions from 2010, I will comment on them with reference to their relevance in 2018. To what extent have these issues been addressed and dispatched already? Which of them are still relevant? Are there any new themes not addressed in 2010?

As mentioned earlier, this book was the inspiration for my current PhD journey. The frustration I felt for many years was somewhat mirrored in the writing of these authors, all established, renowned people within our church. What I want to do is to review the 2010 contributions and cast an "opinion" based on where we are as I see it in 2018 but also informed by my studies to date (now six years) along with taking the view from *my* Ireland. They cover a range of topics from accountability, legality of the concept of PM, issues around HR, the psychological side, life issues for priests, and existing programs and proposals around PM.

Many of the papers in the book address the issue of "accountability" in the church[9] with many references and justifications as to its requirement by canon law, so let us accept that it is in canon law and must be part of "religious" life (using my definition again). The issue is more about "how" that happens, in what context, and more importantly, are religious being held accountable? One point I would make on this word, *accountability*, I feel it has the same negative connotations as does "Performance Management," so a deeper understanding of what is required will help effect change. As is pointed out, there is much discussion and disagreement around this word from within the religious, at some point we must "do."

Reference is made to an existing church model around communication, consultation, and collaboration and is discussed in depth by Wuerl.[10] He also makes the following point:

> While it is important to manage effectively and responsibly the many institutional aspects
> of the Church and her ministry, we can only do this fruitfully with a clear understanding of
> how different the Church is from any other reality we experience, even though the Church
> in her spiritual and pastoral ministry relies on the organizational and managerial skills
> and expertise required to carry out her work in a structured manner.[11]

As I have already stated my intention to focus on hat number 2, being their role as managers (functional role), the above passage supports my decision to first understand "why" and also the need for "organizational and managerial skills and expertise" rather than just impose a solution or request they participate without prior involvement in the design and execution.

The first part of the book covers the performance evaluation of the laity in the church and many excellent ideas and details of programs underway. An obvious issue is that not all are participating, and again this comes back to the unified leadership support from the hierarchy. I note that most of this evidence is survey-based, which is understandable when you have access to a large test group. Quantitative research is perfectly appropriate when you have sufficient numbers, you know what you are attempting to test, and what questions you want to ask. In contrast to the work conducted in 2010, where the researchers were able to use quantitative methods, in my work the questions that need to be asked and answered are not ones that can be answered using survey design. Later, yes, but at this stage, interpretive qualitative work is needed.

Standard PM (define/evaluate, communicate/improve and reward[12]) along with evaluation systems takes up much time for religious, time a lot of them do not have. Canon law now requires that parish administrators observe the principles of church and civil law when dealing with employees, expertise that only a trained qualified person in HR can have. Again, where do they find the time, as many parish administrators are still parish priests?

Considerable effort is being made by some within the church to introduce systems to raise the level of professionalism of the laity that work or volunteer for the church. While this will take time, progress is being made. I believe this itself will cause problems in the relationship between the religious and the laity that work with and for them. Where the laity operate to a higher standard than the religious as they perform their duties, religious do not have the necessary training to operate as an effective leader/manager in their management role. Another theme was that the "wheel" is constantly being reinvented at the parish level when it comes to PM, including performance evaluation. I appreciate that the numbers concerned are large, but a way to avoid this should be possible especially with diminishing resources.

In the second part of the 2010 volume, the emphasis is on the religious themselves. Beal notes that evaluation is mainly done by observation or reports from other religious, confreres aware of their strengths and weaknesses, and so on.[13] I accept that has been the way of the church, but I believe this way to be problematic in that I see it as subjective, and we have many examples demonstrating that this does not work. He also notes that religious generally have no management training, yet they spend a considerable time managing. Beal also makes the important point that in older times each priest would serve time as an apprentice under a more experienced priest, thus learning the trade over an extended period of time, but with less availability of priests, they are put into roles without the proper training.[14] Understandable, but putting religious in roles without the necessary experience or training where that can negatively affect their brothers and the laity around them is inexcusable. Again, referring to my above comment, I understand that resources can be an issue, but in this case, what arises is that in trying to fix one problem, another is created! There are other solutions but, as Beal points out, the biggest barrier to change is the religious themselves citing many reasons, such as lack of time, they did not sign up for this, no interest, to name a few.

A common thread in the second part is the discussion of PM, performance evaluation and assessment, from the position of the religious wearing both hats at the same time; hat 2, the management role, needs nurturing in a different way than hat 1. The removal of any assumed threat to hat 1 would be no longer relevant in this ongoing argument. As competent managers, I believe it would also allow them to influence their work under hat 1, giving them much-needed time and space to do what they say they want to do, what they signed up for.

Following are some of the other points raised that I believe are worth mentioning: "Church leaders at all levels seem to have gotten the message that financial accountability and transparency are important."[15] That may be so, but getting the message and understanding the full implications of that message are not the same. You cannot expect people to see solutions to problems in a field they do not stand in. Seminarians receive considerable training and coaching for hat 1, why not hat 2?

A general theme was the excellent work being done, albeit with limited acceptance, in trying to address lay involvement in our church first before really dealing with the religious—all successful change comes from the inside out or top down. We need to help (and again I deliberately use that word) our religious first. It will make the "outside" piece easier. Religious cannot expect the laity to change first, that's a case of "do as I say, not as I do."

"The Church is not a business."[16] Many thousands of pages have been written on this subject, and I do not intend to join the argument. Suffice it to say that business is part of church life. Simply put, we are talking about the management of people, that word *people* includes the managers themselves.

In summary, my journey actually started with this book. All the authors, I feel, agree on the principle of PM (albeit from slightly different points of view), which is very much based on accountability, the need for HR policies and procedures, and the establishment of standards and competencies "to ensure that all of its resources are used as effectively as possible to carry out God's work on earth."[17] In part 2, the justification for PM within canon law is examined along with the appraisal of seminarians and it being limited to the early years after ordination.[18] Yes, PM is a "tool kit" but it should not be used for discipline or termination of the clergy. "Its purpose is to facilitate learning."[19]

I do not disagree in general terms with most of what has been written, but a few final observations: The word *management* is used 152 times in the book, but no definition is forthcoming! We all have our own idea of what management is, and who are good managers and who are bad. Some more formal agreement is required on the identification of these two positions, "good" and "bad." An accepted understanding of what management is for the religious would remove ambiguity—a source of much trouble in our church.

For me it's not just about imposing systems "to ensure that all of its resources are used as effectively as possible."[20] but "understanding why and how," is a critical first step, not "telling" religious here are the problems and here is the PM "tool kit" solution. Work with them to understand how they do what they do, that they are not "materialistic concepts" or "un-Christian." Let them be part of the proposed solution. This does not remove control from the church but allows for all religious to work from the same page—not saying that everything on that page is right! Alphen refers to this when he talks about "articulating a conceptual framework to facilitate alignment of priest's performance," working from the same page.[21]

Management Role: Many definitions are available but a simplistic one defined by Mintzberg describes the job in terms of "roles" or "organized sets of behaviors identified with a position."[22]

Where We Are Now

I will conclude my discussion by summarizing where we are now. What did we learn in 2010? What is similar and different in 2018? How can a focus on religious' understanding of their management role/what management is, underpin a fit-for-purpose approach to PM in 2018? And finally, bringing us back to the purpose of this gathering, I will comment on how my research contributes to this new aim of identifying new pastoral ways to proclaim the gospel in a changing world. I look forward very much to contributing to this community of research, exchange, and development of fresh solutions to church management challenges.

I still do not believe the church and its leaders understand what to do. It is in our Irish DNA to fight when we feel oppressed by a nation, or in this case the Catholic Church, and intended or not, that is the perception. This is mainly due to the continuing discovery of ongoing scandals that were formerly covered up; all are extremely difficult for many Christians here to accept. The church has gone from being a leader to being an obstruction or blockage in the daily lives of ordinary people. Too many hide behind hat 1 (spiritual hat).

Simply put, I believe the problems were mainly caused by hat 2 (management hat). Without the necessary skill set—competencies to deal with what are primarily management issues: communication, consultation, accountability, ethical/moral behavior—their solution is to fall back and use hat 1 to try to deal with the problem. This does not work.

My Performance Management Principles

The principles below, again under development, come from my work history, my studies, the book I based this paper on, and all the other literature that I have read, especially Armstrong's handbook.[23] Over many years, his work has developed a holistic approach that I very much relate to, a combination of checklists, staying on the path, and level of the bar that I believe should be used. I am trying to stick to ten, as that is the number of my personal life principles. Management principles should

1. Be part of the natural process of management (hat 2)

2. Be a set of "tools" ingrained, reinforced, reviewed, and developed over time

3. Be about managing yourself and the people around you, never losing sight of your moral guidelines

4. Further the objectives of the faith and the church and its ethical guidelines

5. Adhere to the faith, and the laws of God and man

6. Focus on our behavior, personal development, and well-being

7. Acknowledge that gains come from success

8. Be part of the culture—it's what we do!

9. Include mutual respect, procedural fairness, and transparency

10. Have as a lifelong goal to reach the unobtainable "bar"

Conclusion

Following several forays over the last three years into the literature of PM[24] and building a considerable library, I now believe that offering a solution to what I see as a problem was premature in the process and highlighted two main issues. First, imposing a range of solutions on a system purely on the basis of successes in the corporate world, which to many are similar—they both involve people, both have a leadership hierarchy, both have organizational goals, both have or should have a strategy to survive and to help reach those goals, both want to look after their people and adhere to the laws of the land—but the "why" of these organizations is different. Second, all participants cannot become specialists in a field like HR or finance, but they can become better managers. How we apply PM principles to the church is what matters, and to do this we must first understand the difference so we can modify the selection and implementation of PM concepts. Many religious are trying to change the system, but the change needs to come from the top. To quote Beal, "It is clericalism in its many and sometimes subtle forms that poses the greatest obstacle to introducing systems of clergy performance management,"[25] a problem common to many organizations but possible to overcome—possible but not easy! Berlinger acknowledges the difficulty some religious have accepting feedback from a lay source they perceive as not having the right or the knowledge to do this.[26] This is understandable, but it's an example of where the two hats need to be separated so when "understood," feedback would be seen for what it is—only relating to hat 2. Berlinger rightly points out that PM is "just tools from the discipline of management." In Zech's summary and conclusion,[27] he refers to the problems associated with introducing PM in any form on a wide scale within the church and is not optimistic about adoption of PM systems any time soon. It does look as if this statement is still true today, despite heroic efforts in some areas of the church. Maybe a new look, a new approach would aid progress.

Reflection

As I have already stated, I appreciate that the above description of PM that I am developing is a lofty pursuit, but I see no threat to the individual or the church in this definition. I believe that given the correct approach, progress is possible using the principles of PM. Church leaders should be holding the bar of PM above their own heads and not at their waists. We need to ensure the competency and well-being of all religious and adherence to the laws of God, the guiding principles and ethos of the church, while adhering to the laws of the land along with all the rights of all the people whether inside or outside our church. Is that not all that is asked of us? The responsibility for this task lies with the leaders of the church.

This practical reality leads me to believe that the missing step, "being a better manager," will allow religious to conceptually separate their "two hats" and consider the true advantages of PM concepts for our church. I am only one small member of the laity, but from where I stand in Ireland, there needs to be a visible line drawn by the hierarchy and a focus on the present with the aim of "helping" religious now. New numbers are almost nonexistent, and to draw on an analogy from the corporate world, the first thing a company does to attract new employees is to improve the image of the company, review its strategy to make sure they are still on the right path, address its failings and look after the well-being of its existing workforce. My apologies for my lack of understanding of the "calling" to a religious vocation. I have no doubt that many people out there have a desire to devote their lives to the church, but given the choice, would you at this time? There are many paths to follow.

As Dr. Stephen R. Covey says, "Seek first to understand, then to be understood."[28]

Appendix A: Definition of *Religious*

Religious life is open to women and men, while priesthood is open only to men. Women religious are often called sisters or nuns. Men religious can be either be priests or brothers. Brothers are full members of their religious communities and can do any type of ministry—such as teaching—except administering the sacraments, for example, celebrating Mass. Some of the main differences between religious life and the diocesan priesthood are that religious take vows of poverty, chastity, and obedience, they live in community, and they have a defining spirituality and unique mission from their founder or foundress (such as St. Francis). Diocesan priests, on the other hand, don't take the same vows as religious (such as poverty), live in community, or have a distinctive spirituality from their founder. Diocesan priests serve the bishop and people of a given diocese or area of the church. Usually, they serve in the parishes of their diocese under the direction of the diocesan bishop. Their ministry centers around the administration of the sacraments (saying Mass, performing baptisms, weddings, funerals, and hearing confessions). The ministry of diocesan priests is essential to the life of the church since they are the ones who lead and offer sacramental ministry in our parishes. There is no church without parishes and the sacraments. One diocesan priest I know referred to diocesan priests as the general practitioners of the clergy and compared religious to specialists. As in medicine, the church needs both. So, while for the most part diocesan priests serve in parishes, religious can serve in a variety of ways according to the "charism," or unique vision and mission of their founder. That might be in schools, hospitals, orphanages, missions, retreat houses, social justice centers, or other ministries in accordance with the inspiration, special vision, mission, and spirituality of their founder.[29]

Appendix B: Pastoral Responsibilities

Pastoral Responsibilities: To quote an anonymous academic source within an order, on writing down the list of duties involved in "pastoral responsibilities,"

There is as such no list from the Order. If the "flock" were sheep, there could be a list, but the "flock" in question are human beings and, just like parenting, the list of duties involved cannot be quantified and they extend, in particular, beyond the boundaries of this present world. It is precisely this dimension that leads to the whole question necessarily being outside what can be quantified in the context of a "normal" business venture and that makes the topic you are studying unique in relation to "normal" business.

Assumptions

I am assuming that my faith, my church, and my God have no objections to developing ways to be used by religious (according to my definition) throughout their lives in order to ensure a level of mental and physical stability, well-being, and happiness as they follow their path, living out what they believe is their "calling" in a way that is acceptable to their God, the church, and the laws of the land. Then when diversity hits, as it does in life, they have the knowledge, support, and skills training that will allow them to overcome and continue on their path.

Notes

1. Charles E. Zech, ed., *Best Practices in Catholic Church Ministry Performance Management* (Lanham, MD: Lexington Books, 2010).
2. Zech, *Best Practices*.
3. John Beal, "Performance Management of Catholic Clergy: 'Best Practice' or New Iconoclasm?" in Zech, *Best Practices*, 57–70.
4. Zech, *Best Practices*.
5. Michael Armstrong and Angela Baron, *Managing Performance: Performance Management in Action* (London: Chartered Institute of Personnel and Development, 2005).
6. Zech, *Best Practices*.
7. Armstrong and Baron, *Managing Performance*.
8. Armstrong and Baron, *Managing Performance*.
9. See Donald. W. Wuerl, "Framework of Accountability in the Church," in Zech, *Best Practices*, 7–15; Daniel Koys, "Human Resource Guidelines for Developing a Performance Management System," in Zech, *Best Practices*, 19–28. Zeni Fox, "Performance Management in a Family Business?" in Zech, *Best Practices*, 45–53.
10. Wuerl, "Framework of Accountability," 7–15.
11. Wuerl, "Framework of Accountability," 7–15.
12. Koys, "Human Resource Guidelines," 19–28.
13. Beal, "Performance Management of Catholic Clergy," 57–70.
14. Beal, "Performance Management of Catholic Clergy," 57–70.
15. Zech, Introduction, *Best Practices*.
16. Zech, Introduction, *Best Practices*.
17. Zech, Introduction, *Best Practices*.
18. Katarina Schuth, "Importance of Performance Evaluation of Seminarians and Priests for Effective Parish Ministry," in Zech, *Best Practices*, 71–81.
19. Lisa R. Berlinger, "Clergy Performance Management: An Organizational Psychology Perspective," in Zech, *Best Practices*, 83–90.
20. Zech, Introduction, *Best Practices*.

21. James H. Alphen, "Performance Management and Ongoing Formation of Priests," in Zech, *Best Practices*, 91–103.

22. Henry Minitzberg, "The Managers Job Folklore & Fact," *Harvard Business Review* (March–April 1990): 163–76.

23. Michael Armstrong, *Armstrong's Handbook of Performance Management* (London: Kogan Page Ltd., 2018).

24. Such as Armstrong, *Handbook*; Frank Scott-Lennon and Fegus Barry, *Performance Management: Developing People and Performance* (Dublin: Management Briefs Limited, 2008). Armstrong and Baron, *Managing Performance*.

25. Beal, "Performance Management of Catholic Clergy," 57–70.

26. Berlinger, "Clergy Performance Management," 83–90.

27. Zech, Summary and Conclusion, *Best Practices*.

28. Stephen R. Covey, *The 7 Habits of Highly Effective People Personal Workbook* (New York: Simon & Schuster, 2005).

29. Warren Sazama, "Differences Between Religious Life and Diocesan Priesthood," accessed July 7, 2020, https://nrvc.net/ckeditor_assets/attachments/4021/sazama_difference_of_priests.pdf.

11

What Have We Learned?

Charles E. Zech

While not a business, as a human institution the church faces many of the same administrative challenges faced by other organizations. It needs space to meet the needs of its adherents, which means that this space must have working electricity, be heated, and be regularly maintained. Supplies must be purchased. It needs leaders along with paid staff and volunteers on the local, regional, and international levels. In addition to worship, it needs to organize itself to provide services to the poor and oppressed. It needs to plan for the future. The list goes on. All these activities must be conducted within the gospel message of Jesus.

As Rev. Donald Senior, CP, explains in his excellent book *The Gift of Administration*,[1] despite what many believe, the church has always been a human institution in need of organization. For example, Judas was the treasurer (John 13:29). As the early church grew, even more complex organizational structures arose. According to 1 Timothy 5:17–22, elders were put in place. In 1 Timothy 3:1–7, there is a reference to bishops. Acts 6:1–7 speaks of deacons. Acts 11:29–30 tells us of a collection taken up by Paul to financially support Christians in Judea suffering from famine. In fact, Paul identifies administration as one of the gifts given to the church by Christ (1 Cor 12:28).

Over time, the organization of the early church became even more complex. It had to develop organizational structures that would facilitate its sustainability. For example, the first followers met in private homes, but the church outgrew this structure and began adapting other buildings for its use. Later, the church had to respond to the Reformation and the Age of Enlightenment.

The imperative for the church to make the necessary changes in response to changing circumstances continues to this day. While its mission remains the same, the way that mission is carried out must be adapted to the changing world in which the church operates. Any institution, including the church, that fails to adapt will not survive.

In our time, it is not enough to merely adapt. Forces affecting the church are moving so quickly and so dramatically that it must be able to anticipate needed changes and move quickly on them. Adaptation cannot be reactive, it must be proactive, and characterized by out-of-the-box, creative approaches that at the same time promote the church's mission. That is the meaning of good stewardship of church resources today. That is what the individual chapters in this book propose.

If the creative ideas proposed by the chapter authors are adapted, what *will* the church look like in twenty years? How will the entrepreneurial spirit be carried out?

- Decisions will be based on facts and data, not anecdotes or vague impressions.
- The clergy will be formed in pastoral leadership as well as sacramental ministry, with an emphasis on leading the parish in a co-responsible manner.

- Pastors will use the model of the church as the Body of Christ in ministering to a complex group of parishioners, including those with differing ecclesiology, ethnicities, and cultures.

- Parishes will adapt functional business strategies, such as internal financial controls, marketing, and human resource processes to meet the unique situation of a faith-based organization and to become better stewards of the church's resources by using them more efficiently.

- The church will make more effective use of its consultative bodies, such as diocesan synods, pastoral councils, and finance councils to tap into the wealth of talent and creative ideas provided by parishioners.

- The creative ideas that have been implemented will have been based on sound theology, and we will have retained our gospel values.

In Matthew 25:14–30, Jesus provides us with the parable of the talents, which serves as an example of the type of creative management that is needed from church leaders today. The master has gone on a trip and left his resources under the charge of three servants. Those church leaders who make no attempt to be creative in managing church resources are like the servant who buried the talents. Those who try creative approaches but fail to adequately include the laity in a co-responsible manner are like the moderately productive servant. Church leaders who implement creative approaches and involve the laity in a co-responsible way are reflective of the highly productive servant.

All of us, hierarchy, clergy, and laity are called to be adaptive in our efforts to advance the church's mission in the face of changing circumstances. For the church to truly thrive, however, we are also called to be creative. Employing our resources to further the mission of the church in an adaptive and creative manner is the ultimate form of stewardship.

Note

1. Donald Senior, *The Gift of Administration: New Testament Foundations for the Vocation of Administrative Service* (Collegeville, MN: Liturgical Press, 2016).